100 WORKS OF KYOSHI

KYOSHI HYAKKU

Teiko Inabata

Translated by Aya Nagayama and
James W. Henry, III

Trafford
PUBLISHING®

Order this book online at www.trafford.com
or email orders@trafford.com

Most Trafford titles are also available at major online book retailers.

Book cover design by James W. Henry.
Translations by Aya Nagayama and James W. Henry

Printed in Victoria, BC, Canada.

ISBN: 978-1-4251-9093-4

Our mission is to efficiently provide the world's finest, most comprehensive
book publishing service, enabling every author to experience success.
To find out how to publish your book, your way, and have it available
worldwide, visit us online at www.trafford.com/10510

Trafford rev: 1/22/2010

North America & international
toll-free: 1 888 232 4444 (USA & Canada)
phone: 250 383 6864 ♦ fax: 812 355 4082

CONTENTS

Takahama Kyoshi

Acknowledgements
(Aya)

I feel as if I were a little jellyfish floating faintly in the great Ocean of Kyoshi, after I finished translating 100 Works of Kyoshi (Kyoshi Hyakku). The Ocean is so great, so profound, and so thoughtful that the whole process has been beyond my power. It is only the opening step for the world of Kyoshi and it is you who walk into the Kyoshi universe. I appreciate your courageous steps toward our invitation.

I would like to express my sincerest gratitude and appreciation to:

Ms. Teiko Inabata, the author of this book, for having given me this great opportunity.

Dr. Hisashi Inaoka, who has kept giving me good advice and encouragement. Ms. Maureen Wartski, American Author, Haiku-poet, and teacher of writing, who started this translation work with me (from No.4 to No. 19), encouraged me as my best friend and enjoyed reading Kyoshi-sensei. James W. Henry, my wonderful collaborator, American poet and musician, without whom this work would never have been accomplished, and who has done everything necessary for its publication in an English speaking country. I would also like to express my sincerest gratitude to Trafford Publishing Press for publishing this book.

Some years ago, I happened to ask James what he felt about Kyoshi. He immediately answered that Kyoshi was something like water. It sounded very fresh, impressive and unique, and it was instantly understood that James had been able to appreciate and enjoy his study on Kyoshi and his haiku. James explained further that water is as free as to go anywhere it likes, and enriches everything around it, while, on the other hand, water enriches itself by getting nourishment from anything it meets. Kyoshi is as great and free just as this water. Listening to him, hope and optimism were filling my heart instead of worry and anxiety for the future of this book.

James continued to encourage me throughout this long journey of almost ten years, calling me 'Mama Aya.' I would like to give my greatest gratitude and appreciation to my excellent, talented and thoughtful collaborator, James. I also would like to express my heartfelt thanks to my partner of life, Yasutaka, who has been my most helpful friend to share ideas and give feedback whenever I had difficulties or became uncertain of my ability to continue this translation work.

Aya Nagayama, October 9, 2009

ACKNOWLEDGEMENTS

(JAMES)

It has been a remarkable cross-cultural journey for this African American poet/musician (groomed on the likes of Poe, Eliot, Brooks, Pound, Hughes and June Jordan) to be rewarded such intimate exposure to the life and work of Japanese poet Takahama Kyoshi, a stunningly prolific and influential writer, who somehow remains internationally unrecognized, yet is domestically preeminent.

What started out as one-hour English poetry-editing sessions metamorphosed into a joint exploration deeper into the world of haiku than I had imagined. Pre-eminent haiku poet and Japan Traditional Haiku Society founder Teiko Inabata brought Aya Nagayama and me together to this project. Meeting weekly for the past 8 years, Aya and I have had the honor to work with the writings of not one, but two great Japanese literary figures—Teiko and Kyoshi. For me, this has been more educational than even university study, and I am grateful to Teiko to be allowed to contribute to this book, and to Kyoshi's legacy. I also thank her for her peerless hospitality, overflowing generosity, delicious tea and for giving me the fantastic opportunity to speak at the 2007 Haiku Symposium in Ashiya, Japan.

I am especially grateful that Teiko introduced me to the fabulous poet ('Susuki'), mother, grandmother and my newest lifelong friend, Aya Nagayama. Aya has shown an inspired level of dedication to this book, and has sacrificed so much of her time and energy to bring it to life that it inspires awe. She has been the most engaged and engaging partner I could hope to work with, my teacher and my family. We are more than colleagues now, Aya, and it has been a blessing to work with you on such a rewarding endeavor.

I would also like to thank everyone who lent their support and assistance to me in various stages of this 8-year process. Professor June Gordon, whom I met by happenstance in Osaka and whose suggestions and contacts proved invaluable to bringing the publishing task into focus. Our meeting was the happiest of coincidences, and I am grateful to your overwhelming positivity and encouragement while I was feeling around in the dark.

Johnye Strickland of the Haiku Society of America, who generously offered her time and referrals while the project was taking shape. Mr. Jim Kacian of Red Moon Press, whom I was lucky enough to have extended conversation and a few beers with in Tokyo while picking his brain for hints on a potential road map to this book's destination. I sincerely appreciate your guidance and suggestions over the months. Mr. Peter Goodman of Stone Bridge Press was also kind enough to give of his time and insight.

Dr. Hisashi Inaoka was a tireless resource for our translation work from the outset of this project, and Aya and I owe a heartfelt thanks to him for his guidance. He shepherded this project from early on, allowing us the benefit of his expertise and experience in haiku as a professional and a friend.

Aya and I both would like to express our profound appreciation for the assistance of our editor, Ellen D. Beck (Sea Breeze Productions), whose skills and professionalism were an enormous help in getting the material ready for print.

To Trafford staff: thanks to our publishing consultant Angela Aidoo and Author Support representative Dan Culleton, who were both very helpful in getting us set up. Much appreciation to our prepress technician Iryna Artyushenkova for her meticulous technical work and finishing touches. And a very special thanks to Author Support Supervisor Robyn Fraser for being refreshingly attentive, understanding and diligent on behalf of our project. You have been a lifesaver in helping us surmount many minor obstacles to crossing the finish line (on time!).

Much appreciation to Emily Birtwhistle, Ashley Gooch and Leya Taylor for your help with completing the revised version.

To my dear Natalie: although this started before you arrived, you were a great part of the inspiration to complete it.

Finally and most importantly, thanks to my Mom, Verlie McBroom, without whose lifelong support who knows where I'd be.

To new beginnings!

James W. Henry, III
Kobe, Japan
Winter 2009

Introduction to *100* Works of Kyoshi

Little has been written in English about the highly influential haiku poet Takahama Kyoshi (1874-1959). In Japan, the Matsuyama-born disciple of Shiki is practically a household name in literary and poetry circles, not the least for his unquestionable role in creating what we know as modern haiku. Over 100 years after its inception, leading Japanese literary magazine *Hototogisu* ("little cuckoo") remains one among many enduring symbols of Kyoshi's reach. *Hototogisu*, which enjoys a readership of tens of thousands, continues to expand while remaining true to the conservative tenets espoused and represented by Kyoshi (and by extension, his mentor Shiki) through his editorship and teachings.

One of the most important elements of Kyoshi's haiku work is the importance of 'kachoh-fuh-ei' above all. Kachoh-fu-ei can be translated as "to sing of everything in nature, just as birds and flowers." This is believed to encompass both animate and inanimate objects, with equal respect. Another is 'yuki-teikei', which symbolizes the importance of 'kidai', or seasonal words/themes, along with the 5-7-5 phonetic syllable count, in expression of what can be considered true haiku. Inherent in these characteristics of Kyoshi is the rejection of the "new-trend" (non-traditional) haiku movement and its proponents, most notably his contemporary and fellow Shiki protégé, Kawahigashi Hekigotou. The last element of great importance in the work and life of Kyoshi is his eventual embrace of the idea that haiku is the literature of what might be translated as "paradise." Toward the end of his life, images and representations of an almost religious or Buddhist nature began to show up in much of his work, and enlightenment through haiku began surfacing as an underlying theme.

The following essays and selected works are an attempt to give a sense of the understated mastery of Kyoshi's haiku, provide useful insight and historical/biographical context for the writing of the particular pieces and, most importantly, trace the poet's development (or evolution) as exemplified through his work. The ambition and breadth of this project required the diligent research and painstaking care of one of the few writers qualified for such a task, current president of *Hototogisu* and granddaughter of Kyoshi, Teiko Inabata.

- J.H. and A.N.

FOREWORD ON THE TRANSLATION

The translation work of this book has been a labor of love, learning and patience. It has been over seven years since my talented and diligent translation partner, Mrs. Aya Nagayama, and I began working on the material that would eventually form 100 Works of Kyoshi. Our cross-cultural collaboration made attempts at translating the haiku at least a possibility, albeit a distressingly elusive one. (Individually, this arguably would have been an impossible task.) After hundreds of hours of discussion, reading, debate, compromise, deadlock and unexpected epiphany, Aya and I have finally begun to see a flicker of sunlight at the end of our long tunnel.

In my 2007 essay and symposium speech ("Sound, Meaning and Form of Words-Thoughts on Haiku"), I laid out the basis for some of the ways I believe audiences recognize and receive good poetry. It is with these qualities in mind that I sought to work with Aya-san to give life to these wonderful works of Takahama Kyoshi for the benefit of an English-speaking audience. Originally, I was brought to the project as a consultant or proofreader, but I became more involved in the translation aspects as the months progressed and as Teiko Inabata's manuscripts began to take shape as a book. During these early years, as my familiarity with both Japanese culture and Kyoshi's background deepened, so did my interest in and commitment to having the English do some measure of justice to the subject matter—that is, some of the lesser known haiku and biographical narratives of one of the most influential poets of modern Japanese history. The perplexities, nuance and limitations of the Japanese language—not to mention those of the English one--taunted and thwarted us at every turn during the course of this project, so we don't pretend to have achieved all that was demanded, editorially or artistically. In the end, the goal of adapting 100 Works of Kyoshi has been the effort to bring English-speaking and Japanese cultures perhaps a centimeter closer and, as such, is its own reward.

Each of the haiku translations appearing here are the result of hours of rigorous discussion, modification and often, debate. Of the pieces that have been translated elsewhere, many have been interpreted quite differently. Our goal with the material was to adhere as closely as possible to the feeling, the sentiment, the musicality, the biographical context and of course the literal meaning of the original. With this in mind, the reader will find that at times the translation is quite literal, and at others, quite free. Originally we had experimented with a 'literal' and a 'free' translation for each piece. It soon became apparent that the line between the two versions was nearly impossible to draw with any consistency. Generally speaking, nearly all of the pieces required a substantial degree of interpretation to take an English form. More often than not, a *literal* translation would be nonsensical or at best, impenetrable. At times, even impossible. For these reasons, many of the translations contain interpretive elements arrived at through our discussions and editing process.

In the body of this collection, Japanese names are written in Japanese form (surname, followed by given name, e.g., Takahama Kyoshi). However, in the supplementary elements, we have tried to follow Western convention (given name first). Inabata, Nagayama and Henry are all surnames.

Finally, I would like to note that Mrs. Nagayama's grasp of English far exceeds mine of Japanese. In our weekly meetings, innumerable questions were asked to gain the needed insight into Japanese kanji, cultural symbols, historical reference, English vocabulary and so forth. She was always able to digest, respond and question with reliable specificity, and this has been an enormous help to both of us. With time and focussed effort we were able to put forward what we believe to be a considerate and faithful interpretation of these 100 haiku of Takahama Kyoshi.

-J.H.

100 WORKS OF KYOSHI

KYOSHI HYAKKU

No. 1

座を挙げて恋ほのめくや歌かるた

Za o agete koi honomeku-ya uta-karuta

Literal translation:

Romance is kindled
Among all the young gathering –
Uta-karuta

Seasonal word: *uta-karuta*, Japanese playing cards (New Year)

This haiku was written on January 6th, 1906, when Kyoshi was 32 years old.

When we read this haiku, we feel as if we are overhearing carefree, light-hearted, happy laughter of young sophisticates enjoying a New Year's party. Here are Kyoshi's own comments on this haiku:

> Young ladies and gentlemen are playing **uta-karuta**. In this game, people are usually divided into two competing groups, between which the games are played. Some ladies want to be on the same side with certain gentlemen, while other ladies wish to be with others. Only on those occasions of playing **karuta** are they free to express such desires.

From Kyoshi's explanation, we understand that this poem describes a lively party scene with young ladies and gentlemen enjoying *uta-karuta* of *hyakunin-isshu*.

Many poems of *karuta* are love poems. In the days of the Meiji era, and even up to World War II, New Year's parties were the only opportunities for young men and women to meet and enjoy each other's company. Just touching each others' fingers in games was exciting and stimulating. Often romantic feelings were kindled at these New Year's parties.

[Translator's notes about *uta-karuta*: *Uta* means *waka*, a traditional Japanese poem which consists of 31 syllables with the rhythm of 5-7-5-7-7. *Karuta* means Japanese playing cards. When we refer to *uta-karuta*, we usually mean *hyakuninn-isshu*, a set of traditional playing cards with a hundred poems from a hundred ancient poets. This is one of the most popular games played during the New Year holiday.]

According to Kyoshi's postscript for this haiku, the members of the gathering were all gentlemen. This reflects not necessarily what he actually saw but what he remembers. This is very important when you consider the background of this haiku in 1906.

When we talk about the history of modern haiku, Takahama Kyoshi and Kawahigashi Hekigotou are the two most eminent poets. At that time, Hekigotou wrote realistic haiku based on what he actually saw and criticized Kyoshi for writing haiku that were abstract and unreal. Kyoshi's response to this criticism was, in short: "Association and combination of ideas and images are both important and essential in haiku, but *sketching* is also important in creating something that is unique."

With this disagreement lurking in the background, the two took part in a haiku meeting held on the New Year holiday in 1906, like "bitter enemies in the same boat." (See #39)

春風や闘志抱きて丘に立つ

Harukaze ya toushi idakite oka ni tatsu

Literal translation:

On this foothill I stand
Determined and resolute —
Spring breeze

Seasonal word: spring breeze

This haiku was written in 1913, when Kyoshi was 39 years old.

The image of a spring breeze is tranquility, softness, and peacefulness. The cutting word *ya* after the seasonal word, spring breeze, plays a very important role here. Kyoshi is standing in the peaceful spring breeze with strong determination.

For a few years before this haiku was written, Kyoshi preferred to write novels rather than haiku, leaving haiku to Hekigotou, his best friend and famous haiku poet. However, Hekigotou and his followers had gone too far with their new, radical haiku, and Kyoshi thought it a good time to steer haiku back to what he considered its rightful form and content. Kyoshi decided to establish himself as a haiku poet rather than continue as a novelist. He re-initiated the practice of *zatsuei*; that is, selecting the best entries out of all the haiku poems received from <u>Hototogisu</u> subscribers.

As Kyoshi's haiku continued to receive enthusiastic responses from readers, he realized his true calling. He gained pride and self-confidence that he was the true successor of Shiki as a haiku poet. He dedicated himself to selecting the best haiku, as well as finding and encouraging other promising haiku poets. This haiku was written to declare his resolve and fighting spirit under these circumstances.

No. 3

もたれあひて倒れずにある雛かな

Motare-ai-te taorezu ni aru hihina kana

Literal translation:

Without falling down
Leaning on one another
Hina dolls at peace

Seasonal word: *hihina* (*hina*) (spring)

On March 3rd, we Japanese celebrate *hina-matsuri*, the festival of dolls. These are not the dolls small girls play with, but a special set of what are called hina-dolls. The traditional full set consists of more than fifteen figures, including an Emperor and Empress all dressed in ancient Japanese costumes. They are shown on tiered stages with the royal couple at the top. Nowadays, however, the two royal dolls are often substituted for the whole set. Such is the case with this *hina* haiku by Kyoshi. The *hina* dolls here must be a simple standing pair of *hina*. We feel some refined tranquility of the graceful *hina* dolls in this haiku.

The six letters in the first five syllables give the poem a soft, lyrical tone. In haiku, hypermeter usually breaks the rhythm, but this haiku has such a smooth tone that it helps to create the sweet, soft atmosphere suitable to the hina-haiku. Later on, this haiku became one of Kyoshi's favorite haiku of *hina*.

This haiku was written in 1897, when Kyoshi was 24 years old. In this year, the first issue of the haiku periodical Hototogisu was published in Matsuyama in Ehime Prefecture. Kawahigashi Hekigotou and Takahama Kyoshi had become the most distinguished and important haiku poets recognized by Masaoka Shiki.

In that same year, Hekigotou was stricken with smallpox. While he was in the hospital, his fiancée, Ito, left him to be with Kyoshi. Upon learning this, Hekigotou left Tokyo to travel and to try to forget her. In June of that year, Kyoshi and Ito got married. In this haiku, we sense Kyoshi's anxiety about their love and new life.

No. 4

山国の蝶を荒しと思はずや

Yamaguni no chou o arashi to omowazu-ya

Literal translation:

Butterflies are wild
In this mountainous countryside
Don't you think?

On May 14th, 1945, just before World War II ended, Kyoshi, who was living in Komoro, went for a walk with his son Toshio and Tabata Hiko. Kyoshi entertained by hosting an impromptu haiku meeting for the three of them.

In his article entitled "Wild" in the haiku monthly <u>Tamamo</u> (October 1945), run by his daughter Hoshino Tatsuko, Kyoshi wrote about the day this haiku was born. I will quote from it:

> The first impression I had when I came to live in Komoro was that everything here is somehow wild...The next spring, when Toshio and Hiko visited me, we took a walk in the neighborhood. There are slopes wherever we go. If we go up a slope, we go closer to the top of Mt. Asama. On both sides of the slope, there are fields of green wheat and patches of pea-flowers with butterflies flying over the plants. I looked back and said to them, 'Butterflies are wild / In this mountainous countryside / Don't you think?'

No further explanation is needed here, but I would like to add one point: Kyoshi asks Hiko, who came from Kyoto (known for its elegant and refined culture), if he thinks the butterflies in this village are wild. In light of the butterflies they saw, this is the perfect greeting and salutation from Kyoshi to his visitors. It is Kyoshi who maintained the importance of greetings in haiku. This would later develop into the notion that haiku is the poem of *son-mon*, that is, *greeting and addressing.*

No. 5

蛇逃げて我を見し眼の草に残る

Hebi nigete ware o mishi me no kusa ni nokoru

Literal translation:

The snake fled
His eyes that watched me
Were left in the grass

Seasonal word: a snake (summer)

This haiku was written in 1916, when Kyoshi was 42 years old.

Let's imagine Kyoshi encountering a snake in the grass. He was probably scared by it, but at the same time, must have been fascinated by its sparkling green eyes.

After the snake fled, he felt as if there was an afterimage of its green, bewitching eyes still in the grass. Does he show any dislike or fear of the snake? Maybe a little, but I also sense he was in awe of the snake and of nature itself.

This haiku represents not only what Kyoshi actually witnessed in his encounter with the snake but also what he saw in his mind's eye. This poem's origin is in reality and imagination, and contains both objective and subjective descriptions. It not only depicts a scene in nature but also illustrates what he was thinking.

No. 6

主客閑話蝸牛竹をのぼるなり

Shukaku kanwa dedemushi take o noboru-nari

Literal translation:

The host and guest
In tranquil talk;
A snail climbing a bamboo

Seasonal word: a snail (summer)

This haiku was written in 1906, when Kyoshi was 33 years old.

While the host and his guest(s) are enjoying a quiet and peaceful talk, out in the garden a snail is slowly climbing up a bamboo.

This haiku offers us a tranquility that is at odds with the trivialities of life. Where does the feeling come from? Of course, *kanwa* means a quiet talk, but it comes mainly from the description of a snail crawling up a bamboo.

Although there is no direct correlation between human conversation and the snail's movement, the latter gives us a sense of the snail's universe, where time moves slowly and peacefully, untouched by man's reality.

No. 7

大海のうしほはあれど旱かな

Taikai no ushio wa aredo hideri kana

Literal translation:

The water is deep
In the ocean;
Drought on the land

Seasonal word: drought (summer)

It was written in 1904, when Kyoshi was 31 years old.

The first part of this haiku offers us the image of a blue, blue ocean with a long, sun-splashed coastline. But in the last line we are to turn our eyes to the fields and farms suffering from a spell of dry weather with withering plants and crops. The desolate landscape is all the more heartbreaking because of the beautiful blue sea. Or the sea may be the more beautiful because of the drought-stricken land.

When Kyoshi was a newborn baby, his father decided to become a farmer and tried hard to reclaim land near the Inland Sea for his livelihood. However, he had to give up his life as a farmer after seven years. In his earliest memories, Kyoshi must have had a picture of his father's hard work on the dry, barren farm near the blue sea.

Actually, this haiku was not written near the ocean or on the farm but at a certain haiku meeting. This means that the haiku was not a depiction of a scene but rather drawn out of his early memories. In this case, he sympathizes with the farmers' sorrow which is set so poignantly against the picturesque blue ocean.

No. 8

金亀子擲つ闇の深さかな

Koganemushi nageutsu yami no fukasa kana

Literal translation:

Koganemushi
I hurled it against the night
How deep the darkness

Seasonal word: *koganemushi,* a Japanese gold beetle (summer)

This haiku was written in 1908, when Kyoshi was 34 years old.

Koganemushi is a Japanese beetle, a common summer bug with a green-gold body and wings. This two-centimeter insect buzzes toward a light then suddenly plops down and pretends to be dead. After a while, it flies back to the same light, repeating this maneuver again and again until someone catches it and throws it out the window.

Hurling this beetle into the dark night, Kyoshi realized how rich and dense the darkness was, and became awestruck when the bug he had flung outside seemed to be swallowed up by the fathomless depths of the night. He just stared at the dark nothingness spread out before him.

There used to be a vast, pitch-black darkness around our houses at night, but, sadly, we have lost it. The electric lights of modern civilization have consumed our beautiful night shadows.

No. 9

東に日の沈みゐる花野かな

Hingashi ni hi no shizumi-iru hanano kana

Literal translation:

Still sunk in the east
Is the sun; the field of
Wild flowers

Seasonal word: *hanano*, a field of wild flowers (autumn)

Written in 1915, when Kyoshi was 41 years old.

When you read "the sun is still sunk in the east," you may wonder if you have read it correctly. It is a well known truth that both the sun and the moon rise in the east and sink (set) in the west. Then we notice the qualifier "still" and realize that Kyoshi is talking about dawn. He is describing, in his straightforward way, a personal insight without any a priori views.

The sun has not yet risen, but in dawn's gray light we perceive that a shadowed field stretches before us. Soon the eastern sky will brighten and the field will show itself. It is still gray-green in the half-light, but as the sky becomes lighter we will see innumerable little wildflowers tinged with faint morning light. As the sun rises, these flowers will gradually display their full colorful beauty.

This haiku has a magic that enables all the readers to imagine subtle, moment-by-moment changes that occur in a field of wildflowers in the morning.

No. 10

能すみし面の衰へ暮の秋

Noh sumishi men no otoroe kure no aki

Literal translation:

Noh-play is over
The mask diminishes –
Late in autumn

Seasonal word: *kure-no-aki*, late in autumn

This haiku was written in 1918, when Kyoshi was 44 years old.

The Noh performance is over, and the mask worn during the play now lies on the table.

The mask, which had life and animus on the stage, has reverted to being a simple wooden artifact.

To describe the way in which something is lost from the mask, Kyoshi writes "the mask diminishes." This simple, rather practical expression serves to convey the metaphysical meaning behind it.

Furthermore, by using the words "late in autumn," Kyoshi imbues the haiku with the serenity of that season. He implies that the Noh mask has lost its soul, just as the liveliness of all things in nature ebbs in late autumn.

No. 11

遠山に日の当りたる枯野かな

Tohyama ni hi no ataritaru kareno kana

Literal translation:

The sun shines
On the distant mountains;
Withered field

Seasonal word: *kareno*, withered field (winter)

This haiku was written in 1900, when Kyoshi was 26 years old.

This is one of Kyoshi's most famous masterpieces and is considered a pivotal piece in establishing a haiku world of his own.

It is not difficult to understand this haiku. Far-off mountains are seen across a withered field. The mountains are lit by the glow of the late afternoon sun, whereas in the foreground the winter field lies bleak and desolate.

This haiku deeply moves all who read it. Why does it evoke such a heartfelt reaction? Perhaps it is because the scene is so plainly described. We, the readers, can clearly visualize what Kyoshi saw and superimpose this image over our own memories.

The sun-lit mountains at the end of the bleak winter field may give hope and comfort to all of us life travelers.

冬帝先づ日をなげかけて駒ケ嶽

Tohtei mazu hi o nagekakete komagatake

Literal translation:

God of Winter
Casts his first ray on top of
Mt. Komagatake

Seasonal word: *Tohtei*, God of Winter

This haiku was written in January in 1920, when Kyoshi was 46 years old.

This haiku was written onboard ship while Kyoshi was returning home from Otaru, which is situated in the north of Hokkaido. In Otaru, Kyoshi had been at the bedside of his son Toshio, who was in the hospital with erysipelas. Kyoshi had made this long trip alone because his wife, Ito, was not able to leave home with their six-month-old baby.

Toshio was seriously ill, and Kyoshi was evidently prepared for the worst. Fortunately, Toshio got better and Kyoshi was able to leave Otaru and return home. While he was on the boat for this homeward journey, he saw one peak sharply delineated with gold in the dawn light amidst the shadow of the mountains. Told that this was Mt. Komagatake, Kyoshi interpreted the sight as a favorable message from the god of winter.

The resulting poem was Kyoshi's prayer of thanksgiving for his son's recovery and also an expression of gratitude for the peace he now felt in his heart.

No. 13

時ものを解決するや春を待つ

Toki mono o kaiketsu suru ya haru o matsu

Literal translation:

May time solve
Worries and difficulties –
Awaiting the spring

Seasonal word: awaiting spring, *haru o matu*

This haiku was written in 1914, when Kyoshi was 40 years old.

This haiku shows Kyoshi earnestly waiting for spring while wishing that the passage of time could solve his worries and difficulties. The cutting word *ya* implies his prayerful wishes; "Will time solve all problems?" he asks himself. "I hope so. Still, if this is not to be, I will face what comes."

The haiku does not imply that Kyoshi indulges in negative thought. Rather, it offers his philosophical view of life and shows that he does his best without allowing himself to be torn by anxiety. Time, Kyoshi says, will hopefully provide answers. In other words, he has made his peace with life.

Worried and uncertain about publishing the haiku monthly <u>Hototogisu</u> and his own literary life, he went on a trip to his hometown, Matsuyama. On his way back, Kyoshi had some haiku meetings with his old friends and acquaintances, where he was reassured that haiku was the only road he should follow. This poem offers us a glimpse of his resurgent self-confidence and courage.

No. 14

葛城の神みそなはせ青き踏む

Kazuraki no kami misonawase aokihumu

Literal translation:

Goddess of Mt. Katsuragi;
Please look at us stepping on
Early spring grass

Seasonal word: *aokihumu*, stepping on early spring grass

This haiku was written in 1917, when Kyoshi was 42 years old.

Misonawase is the Japanese honorific word for "to see." It is rather difficult to ascertain the identity of the goddess (or god). The origin of Katsuragi-no-kami lies in Hitokotonushi-no-kami, the god of Mt. Katsuragi, who was said to give his entire message in one word. In early legends, this god was considered to be brave and magnificent, but later on his luster diminished until he became a minor deity.

In a Noh play, Kazuraki-no-kami was transformed into an ugly goddess who hid herself in the darkness of the night. Since Kyoshi was well-versed in Noh, it seems natural to assume that he addresses this goddess in his poem.

Kyoshi's haiku is filled with the joy of stepping onto early spring grass. In this spirit of joy, he calls upon the ugly goddess to leave darkness behind and to enjoy a walk with him, thus offering us a harmonious mix of legend and reality.

No. 15

一つ根に離れ浮く葉や春の水

Hitotsu ne ni hanare uku ha ya haru no mizu

Literal translation:

From a single root
Little green leaves floating aloof;
Spring water

Seasonal word: spring water

This haiku was written in 1913, when Kyoshi was 39 years old.

While taking a walk one day in early spring, Kyoshi came upon a ditch filled with water. As he looked down into it, Kyoshi observed that though the sun sparkled in the water and warmed his back, the east wind still brought a chill to his cheek.

Thinking that spring could surely be felt in the microcosm down in the ditch, Kyoshi threw a pebble into the water. Through the soft mud that floated up like smoke, he saw dark algae at the bottom. Then he noticed a green leaf on the surface of the water. Surely this was a harbinger of spring! Kyoshi realized that the leaf was connected to a stem, and that this stem rose from a submerged root. Observing more closely, he was surprised to find many more stems emerging in a radial fashion from the root, each with a leaf on top.

Perceiving that the entire universe could be seen in this humble plant, he felt it was a true gift of nature and understood how close observation and profound contemplation were linked to each other.

No. 16

草摘みし今日の野いたみ夜雨来る

Kusa tsumishi kyou no no itami yau kitaru

Literal translation:

To cure fields where
We gathered greens in daylight
It rains at night

Seasonal word: *kusatumu*, gathering spring herbs, gathering greens (spring)

This haiku was written in 1913 when Kyoshi was 38 years old.

In an essay about this haiku Kyoshi writes:

> On that day we gathered young greens in a field in Kamakura, and in the night I awoke to hear the sound of rain. Listening to the soft sound, I could imagine that the heavens had sent the rain to cure the fields we had inadvertently damaged by our gathering. Consoled by this thought, I fell back to sleep. This haiku was born at that moment.

Reading the poet's explanation, we can well understand what he meant. There are no difficult words in this poem, and it has a light rhythm that easily touches our hearts. We can feel Kyoshi's sensitive warmth toward nature, and perceive that this haiku shows the animism still hidden in his heart.

We understand that the heavens feel compassion for the spoiled field. We are also relieved and comforted, as if we, too, had listened to the healing rain.

No. 17

白牡丹といふといへども紅ほのか

Hakubotan to iu to iedomo kou honoka

Literal translation:

A *white peony*
We say, yet I sense
Faint pink

Seasonal word: *botan*, a peony

This haiku was written in 1925 when Kyoshi was 51 years old.

In Kyoshi's garden in Kamakura, there were three peony trees, two with scarlet flowers and one with white ones. He especially loved the tree with white peonies. When they were blooming, they enchanted him. Kyoshi thought that while the scarlet peonies had a spellbinding attractiveness, the white peonies were extremely graceful and sublime.

As he continued to admire the white peony, Kyoshi came to realize that the flower's pristine loveliness was heightened by the faintest tinge of pink. This roseate shading enhanced the white blossom's innate charm and grace.

There is a beautiful rhythm in this haiku. It starts with six syllables, which give the poem a soft tone, followed by the seven slow and elegant *hiragana*, which seem to echo the swaying petals of the peony. The subtle tenor of the last five syllables offers us an image of faint but bewitching pink in the heart of the white flower.

No. 18

どかと解く夏帯に句をかけとこそ

Doka to toku natsu-obi ni ku o kaketokoso

Literal translation:

Thud! Taking off her
Summer obi, she asked me
To write haiku on it

Seasonal word: a summer *obi* (sash)

This haiku was written in 1920, when Kyoshi was 46 years old.
Later, Kyoshi wrote this about it:

> One day after our Noh performance, we went to a Japanese restaurant
> in Kamakura to enjoy ourselves over cups of sake. The head waitress,
> who was a little tipsy, untied her obi, dropped it as though it were some-
> thing heavy, and asked me to write a haiku on it.

What makes this poem so excellent is the fact that the first five syllables in
Japanese are unique and audacious. The onomatopoeic adverb *doka-to* (with
a thud) gives us a sense not only of the heavy sash but also of its buxom
wearer. It also portrays the vigorous and awkward movement made by the
plump, tipsy maid.

We are charmed and impressed by the originality of this haiku and by the
way Kyoshi's expressive imagery draws us into this cheerful, lighthearted
scene.

No. 19

大夕立来るらし由布のかきくもり

Oh-yudachi kururashi Yuhu no kaki-kumori

Literal translation:

Great showers are coming-
Mt. Yuhu has been covered
With dark clouds

Seasonal word: *yuhdachi* (or *yudachi*), evening showers[summer]

Written in 1927, when Kyoshi was 55 years old.

On his way back from Beppu, Kyoshi visited the Kijima Plateau at the foot of Mt. Yuhu, where he found that majestic mountain swathed in dark clouds. The air itself was dark and heavy with impending rain.

Note that this haiku conveys a real sense of distance. Kyoshi, who was no doubt standing on the Kijima Plateau (which is blessed with the best view of Mt.Yuhu), indicates the distance between himself and the mountain by expressing his awe at Mt.Yuhu's grandeur.

We are even more inspired, knowing that this is one of the twenty-five haiku entitled "Draught." This was the rain people had long been awaiting.

No. 20

桐一葉日当りながら落ちにけり

Kiri hitoha hiatari-nagara ochinikeri

Literal translation:

A paulownia leaf
Is falling down with
Sunshine on it

Seasonal phrase: a falling leaf of paulownia tree, *kiri-hitoha*, (early autumn)

This haiku was written on August 27, 1906, when Kyoshi was 32 years old.

The origin of the phrase "a leaf of the paulownia tree" is traced back to classical Chinese literature. This phrase alludes to the loneliness of early autumn when all living things begin to decline.

In Kyoshi's haiku, a big paulownia leaf is falling slowly earthward. In the middle seven syllables of the Japanese haiku, Kyoshi shows how the broad leaf glides down to earth, reflecting early autumn sunlight. The sun-splashed leaf spirals down as if in slow motion, and we are entranced. Then, in the last five syllables, it sinks silently to the ground.

By using such vivid imagery, Kyoshi not only shares a memory with us but succeeds in giving new life to a classic phrase.

No. 21

子規逝くや十七日の月明に

Shiki yuku ya juh-shichi nichi no getsumei ni

Literal translation:

Shiki passed away —
In serene light of the moon
Of seventeen days old

Seasonal word: the moon

Kyoshi wrote this famous haiku of mourning and condolence on the occasion of Shiki's death. Shiki died in the early morning hours of September 19, 1902. He was thirty-six years old, and Kyoshi was twenty-eight.

In his memoirs Kyoshi wrote:

> That night everybody went home, and I alone stayed with him (Shiki). I did not feel like sleeping, and around midnight I went out into the garden. The beautiful moon was up in the sky above the gourd trellis, and as I stood looking at it, my heart was filled with an ineffable emotion.

Soon afterwards, Kyoshi goes on to say, Shiki's mother called him to say that Shiki had passed away.

When Kyoshi went out the gate to tell Hekigotou and Sokotsu about Shiki's death, he noticed that the seventeen-day-old moon seemed even brighter than before. Kyoshi mused that it was as though the departed soul of Shiki were ascending into the sky. Almost involuntarily the poem sprang to his lips.

This haiku, which was created so spontaneously, is nevertheless both solemn and refined and reflects the poet's affection and reverence for Shiki.

No. 22

この松の下に佇めば露の我

Kono matsu no shita ni tatazumeba tsuyu no ware

Literal translation:

Standing under
This pine tree
I am a drop of dew

Seasonal word: Dew (autumn)

When Kyoshi was 43 years old, he prefaced this haiku by writing as follows: "When I went to my hometown, I visited Nishinoge in Kazahaya, where I had spent the first eight years of my life. My old house was gone and there remained only a small temple on the bank of the river. By this temple stood the old pine tree."

Standing under the old pine tree, Kyoshi may well have recalled those who, like his parents, had passed away. He may have thought of other people who had once been an important part of his life. Since all that remained of his childhood was this one pine tree, a sense of transience must have settled deeply into Kyoshi's heart, leaving him feeling that he, too, was as ephemeral as the dew.

This scene, and the thoughts and feelings it evoked, apparently inspired Kyoshi throughout his life. In his haiku and essays he often refers to the pine tree. This particular haiku is therefore the key to our understanding Kyoshi's "haiku cosmos."

No. 23

二三子や時雨るる心親しめり

Nisan-shi ya shigururu kokoro shitashimeri

Literal translation:

A few people –
Sharing appreciation of
Winter light shower

Seasonal word: *shigure*, light winter early shower

Shigure is a heartfelt seasonal word. It is the rain that ushers us into winter. It rains for a brief time and then stops soon afterward. When the clouds pass, the sun shines. Sometimes it rains amid sparkling sunshine.

Kyoshi had attended the third memorial ceremony of his eldest brother's death in his hometown, Matsuyama. There he wanted to see Seigetsu, one of his old haiku friends, but he was unable to because Seigetsu was also in mourning for his mother.

Kyoshi wrote this haiku in Sakai on his way home from Matsuyama, when he had a haiku gathering with his old friends. Kyoshi's heart must have been filled with loneliness, missing those who had passed. It must have been lightly raining outside. Among those gathered were some who could understand Kyoshi's heart and regarded the drizzling rain as something dear and precious.

No. 24

大空に伸び傾ける冬木かな

Ohzora ni nobi katamukeru fuyu-ki kana

Literal translation:

A winter tree;
Stretching and leaning
Into the great sky

Seasonal word: a winter tree

This haiku was written in 1926, when Kyoshi was 53.

A big tree, having lost all its leaves, stands in utter silence. If one looks up at the tree from beneath, however, one beholds a sturdy trunk stretching and spreading high up into the great sky, leaning modestly near the top.

If the poem is read in one breath, the rhythm sounds as muscular as the strong trunk of a big tree. At the end, the poetic flow is stopped suddenly and dramatically by the cutting word *kana*, and great echoes are left thereafter. In this way, the simple vision of a big winter tree is enhanced and becomes symbolic.

No. 25

凍蝶の己が魂追うて飛ぶ

Itechou no onoga tamashii oute tobu

Literal translation:

A frozen butterfly
Will fly after
Its own soul

Seasonal word: a frozen butterfly, *ite-chou*, (winter)

This haiku was written on January 26, 1933, when Kyoshi was 60 years old.

Kyoshi explains that *ite-chou* is a butterfly that survives the winter. It lies weak and semi-dormant in the shade, but when touched by the warmth of the sun, its wings flutter weakly and it begins to fly. Kyoshi says he had the impression that the spirit of the seemingly lifeless butterfly is the first to take wing and that the body then flies to overtake its soul.

Kyoshi succeeds in describing the fragile winter butterfly as a beautiful and transcendent soul. There is also a connection to Noh plays, in which he was deeply versed. In Noh, dancing (*mai*) is commonplace. Even though a theme might be tragic, the hero (*shite*) performs a dance. It is through this dance that the audience realizes that the hero's soul will find peace in a celestial afterlife.

As in Noh, Kyoshi has transformed the feeble dance of a frozen butterfly into a spiritual image that evokes eternity. In 1933, Kyoshi had not yet written his theory that haiku is "a literature of paradise (*gokuraku-no-bungaku*)." However, the idea must have been in the depths of his mind. With this haiku, Kyoshi must have literarily saved the frozen butterfly and transformed it into an eternal and celestial frozen butterfly.

紅梅の紅の通へる幹ならん

Kohbai no koh no kayoeru miki naran

Literal translation:

Through the trunk of
This plum tree of red blossoms
Crimson must be running

Seasonal word: *ume*, Japanese red plum blossoms (spring)

This haiku was written in March 1931, when Kyoshi was 57.

The literal meaning of this haiku is as follows: Crimson plum blossoms are blooming. A close look at the tree shows that its trunk seems tinged with red. According to Kyoshi, it is as if crimson was running through the body of the tree.

This haiku, I feel, is Kyoshi's dedication to the plum tree. When he beheld it with his heart, he felt that the essence (spirit) of the red plum tree was coursing through its trunk.

Kyoshi had been brought up with the belief that all of nature was sentient. He thought it perfectly natural that trees should talk, feel emotion, or express enjoyment. His connection with nature was partly instinctive, partly due to his childhood study, and partly due to the influence of Noh, in which he was extremely well-versed.

Kyoshi understood the elegant simplicity of all natural things, not scientifically but in his own poetic way.

No. 27

木々の芽のわれに迫るや法の山

Kigi no me no ware ni semaru ya nori no yama

Literal translation:

All the buds on the trees are
Rushing toward me –
At this Mountain of Buddhist Temple

This haiku was written in March 1927, when Kyoshi was 54 years old.

The meaning of this haiku must be as follows: when I entered the main gate of the Buddhist temple and was looking quietly at the buds of the trees, they seemed as if they were surging towards me.

What is unique about this poem is the strange and overwhelming power of the life sprouted in trees in spring and its indelible impression on Kyoshi's mind (and on ours, as well). It is obvious that Kyoshi thought all trees and plants had life as we do, and that he looked at nature with an animistic point of view.

Kyoshi writes in one of his books that when our mind is familiar with the flowers and birds we watch, it absorbs them, and they come to move as our mind moves and feel as our mind feels.

In this way, we express our own minds by delineating the colors and the shapes of what we see.

This is the essence of what he would introduce the following year as *kyakkan shasei*, that is, objective sketch.

No. 28

咲き満ちてこぼるゝ花もなかりけり

Saki michite koboruru hana mo nakari-keri

Literal translation:

Cherry blossoms
In full bloom –
No petals falling

Seasonal word: cherry blossoms, *hana* (spring)

Kyoshi wrote this haiku, considered to be one of his most important poems, in April, 1926. He was fifty-four years old.

In this serene haiku Kyoshi writes about the stillness of cherry blossoms in full bloom. So still are these flowers, Kyoshi writes, that not even a petal falls.

In Japan, the cherry blossom is nationally extolled. Cherry blossoms are thought to be glorious, proud, and ephemeral. Now Kyoshi offers us yet another facet of this beloved tree: cherry blossoms that flower in motionless grace. The loveliness of this hush, this absolute stillness of cherry blossoms in full bloom, makes us catch our breath.

No. 29

人間吏となるも風流胡瓜の曲がるも亦

Ningen ri to naru mo fuhryuh kyuuri no magaru mo mata

Literal translation:

Poetic is to be
A public servant, so are
Crooked cucumbers

Seasonal word: a cucumber (summer)

This haiku was written 1917, when Kyoshi was 43 years old.

The meaning of this haiku is that we may think it refined for a person to be a civil servant, just as we believe this cucumber to be poetic because it is crooked.

I said *this* cucumber because he wrote another haiku with the same seasonal word (cucumber) on the same occasion. Kyoshi and Seiran, to whom this haiku is dedicated, seem to be munching cucumbers at the time, some of which are crooked. They are exchanging greetings each other, expressing their friendship with a little bit of fun and irony.

It is obvious that this haiku is out of rhythm, as it consists of twenty-three syllables. Kyoshi was very strict about the fundamental theory that haiku should have seventeen syllables and a seasonal word. Actually, however, there are quite a few extra-syllable haiku among his works, especially at this time of his life.

No. 30

飛騨の生れ名はとうといふほととぎす

Hida no umare na wa tou to iu hototogisu

Literal translation:

Born in Hida
Girl's name is "Tou"
Hototogisu

Seasonal word: *Hototogisu*, a Japanese cuckoo (summer)

This haiku was written in 1931 when Kyoshi was 57 years old.

The repetition of the [t] sound in the latter half of this haiku gives it its charming rhythm and evokes the song of the cuckoo, which we typically interpret as an onomatopoeia "teppen-kaketaka."

Kyoshi writes an engaging story about this haiku. While he was staying in Kamikochi, where the sound of *hototogisu*, a Japanese cuckoo, could be heard night and day, a brown-cheeked country girl served him at dinner time. When Kyoshi asked her name, she answered, "Tou." The name sounded rather unique, so he asked her to repeat it, and she abruptly repeated, "Tou!" He then asked where she had been born, and she answered that she had been born in Hida, a small village surrounded by high mountains.

On the day of Kyoshi's departure, Tou accompanied him down the mountain. He then advised her to go back, and waved goodbye to her with his Panama hat. She also waved goodbye, and they parted.

The ingenuous and unspoiled character of this girl made Kyoshi nostalgic for the *hototogisu* and the fresh mountain air; hence, this tender haiku was born.

No. 31

神にませばまこと美はし那智の滝

Kami ni maseba makoto uruwashi nachi no taki

Literal translation:

Beheld as divinity
How sublime is
The Nachi waterfall

Seasonal word: *taki*, waterfall (summer)

Written in 1933, when Kyoshi was 59.

This haiku was actually composed on April 10th, in 1933, when Kyoshi visited Nanki, which is the name of the southern part of Wakayama-prefecture. But "waterfall" is a seasonal word of summer, so I decided to present this haiku for July.

Kyoshi climbed all the way from Katsuura, looking up at the waterfall from a distance. When he finally stood in front of this Nachi waterfall, he found it far beyond what he had imagined in his mind. Kyoshi was overwhelmed by its divine magnificence and colossal pillars of water.

He might have been stricken speechless for a while by the awesome beauty of the fall and seemed to be almost assimilated into the fall itself. I think it was only after he regained his senses that this haiku was born out of his deep emotion.

This haiku sounds like a symphony enlivened by a superb spirit, rather than merely a sketch of the waterfall.

No. 32

燈台はひくく霧笛は峙てり

Tohdai wa hikuku muteki wa sobadateri

Literal translation:

Lighthouse sits low;
While foghorn towers
To the sky

Seasonal word: fog (autumn)

Written in 1933, when Kyoshi was 59.

In August 1933, Kyoshi visited Kushiro in Hokkaido. At the southern end of the town was a white lighthouse that was smaller than he had expected. Next to the lighthouse, however, stood a tall foghorn tower that was much higher than the lighthouse. A foghorn is a steam whistle that lets the ships know their location in a dense fog. The Kushiro harbor is famous for its thick fog. Lost in this fog, the lighthouse is rendered useless.

This haiku is, of course, the sketch of the not-so-tall lighthouse and the big foghorn next to it. But when I read it, I am struck by the fact that the sound of the foghorn can penetrate the dense fog when even the strong light of the lighthouse cannot.

I think Kyoshi wanted to communicate the pathos he felt at this lonely harbor in the northern sea as well as the deep solitude of the journey.

No. 33

ふるさとの月の港をよぎるのみ

Hurusato no tsuki no minato o yogiru nomi

Literal translation:

Only passing
This harbor of moonlight
So near my old hometown

Seasonal word: the moon (autumn)

This haiku was written in 1928, when Kyoshi was 54.

On the night of October 4th, 1928, Kyoshi boarded a ship at Takamatsu for Beppu. This trip took him thirteen hours. Around two o'clock in the morning, the ship docked at Takahama harbor, which was located only six kilometers from his hometown, Matsuyama.

Kyoshi is standing on the deck and watching the quiet harbor glow in the clear moonlight. There are no shadows or lights from the houses, only moonlight reflected off their shiny silver roof tiles. Behind them is the black silhouette of the mountains in his dear old hometown. The sea in front of him looks peaceful, the waves twinkling in the light of the moon. All is silent, all is clear.

His heart must be filled with a variety of emotions: nostalgia, regret that he is just passing the harbor without visiting his hometown, and joy at reconfirming that his homeland is so beautiful.

Of course, it is Kyoshi who is passing the harbor of the moon, but we feel as if he himself were the moon crossing the harbor near his hometown.

No. 34

椀ほどの竹生島見え秋日和

Wan hodo no chikubu-jima mie akibiyori

Literal translation:

Beautiful autumn day
Chikubu Island appears small
Like a wooden soup bowl

Seasonal word: beautiful autumn day, *akibiyori*

Written in 1936, when Kyoshi was 61 years old.

Chikubujima is a small island in the northern part of Lake Biwa. Generally speaking, *kohoku*, the district on the northern outskirts of the lake, is rather quiet and lonely. People living there are traditional and religious, maintaining a provincial culture of their own.

When I first read this haiku, I thought it was meant to express what the little island looked like on a fine autumn day. However, upon deeper consideration, I came to realize it was the other way around—Kyoshi was actually praising the beautiful autumn day itself by describing how clearly the little island appeared from a distance.

Kyoshi often said that haiku are poems that "sing" on seasonal words. This haiku is a good example of what he meant.

No. 35

流れゆく大根の葉の早さかな

Nagare-yuku daikon no ha no hayasa kana

Literal translation:

Downstream flow
Leaves of Japanese radish –
How fast they go!

Seasonal word: washing white Japanese radish, *daikon arau*.

Written in November 1926, when Kyoshi was 54 years old.

This haiku is regarded as an ideal example of a haiku of objective sketch.
Kyoshi himself once writes about this haiku as follows:

> I was walking along the River Tama one day in the early winter. Looking
> at colored leaves, walking through *susuki* grass blown down by the wind,
> passing by withered trees with some ripened red persimmons in a farm-
> house yard, I happened to come across a brook and watched the water
> flowing from a bridge. I saw some green leaves of white Japanese radish
> (*daikon*) flowing so quickly. This haiku was born at that moment. I be-
> came mesmerized by the powerful image of the green leaves, and other
> previous images carried in my heart were temporarily forgotten.

How simple and casual his sketch is. We have to remember, however, that it
is borne of his pure spiritual and artistic focus.

We also should not forget how effective the seasonal word "washing rad-
ish, *daikon arau*'" works here, which vividly reminds us of women washing
muddy *daikon* in the stream, their lives, and winter scenery around the River
Tama.

No. 36

静けさに耐へずして降る落葉かな

Shizukesa ni taezu shite furu ochiba kana

Literal translation:

Under weight of
Unbearable tranquility
Winter leaf falls

Seasonal word: winter leaf, dead leaf, fallen leaf (winter)

Written in 1937, when Kyoshi was 63 years old.

In the quietness of the mountain without even a bird singing, winter leaves are ready to fall from the branches if something happens to invite them. But nothing happens.

There is utmost quietness. At last, a leaf falls, unable to bear the overwhelming tranquility.

Kyoshi closely identifies with nature, sharing a bond which becomes stronger and stronger until it is as if he himself becomes the leaf. Thus, amidst the broken tranquility, Kyoshi's heart is the falling leaf, no longer able to sustain its own weight.

I had the same experience when I visited Komoro, where Kyoshi lived, after the end of the world war II. I was standing near a lonesome shrine. It was quiet for a while, and in the next moment leaves suddenly started falling. Instantly, I thought of Kyoshi.

No. 37

日ねもすの風花淋しからざるや

Hinemosu no kazahana sabishi-karazaru ya

Literal translation:

*Light snow fluttering
In the sky all day long –
Isn't it so lonesome?*

Seasonal word: light fluttering snow, *kazahana*

This was written in January 1937, when Kyoshi was 63 years old.

Reading this haiku, my heart is filled with sympathy for the deep loneliness of the people who live in Niigata. Niigata, a city in the northern part of Japan on the side facing the Japan Sea, is famous for its heavy snow. Once it starts snowing, it keeps snowing for days. The above haiku is one of the five haiku Kyoshi wrote during a special haiku gathering held in that city.

This feeling of deep loneliness comes from the seasonal word *kazahana*. *Kazahana* means light snowflakes, beautiful but ephemeral, sometimes twinkling with sunlight and sometimes dark in the shadows. I think this haiku expresses Kyoshi's sympathy and pity for the lonely, dreary life in the snowy country.

However, that is not all. It also expresses his greeting and encouragement for Mizuho and Sujuh, two great poets of <u>Hototogisu</u> who were professors at Niigata University of Medical Science. This is a *sonmon-no-ku* for the two prominent poets.

No. 38

古綿子着のみ着のまま鹿島立

Huru watako kinomi kinomama kashimadachi

Literal translation:

Donning mere
Everyday old quilted jacket
I set out on my journey

Seasonal word: *watako*, a quilted jacket (winter)

Written on February 16, 1936, when Kyoshi was 62.

In the preface of this haiku, Kyoshi wrote, "On the Hakone-maru at Yokohama harbor, at three o'clock in the afternoon."

Kyoshi left for Berlin on February 16th 1936, and came back on June 15th. He wrote this haiku in his cabin right after he said goodbye to a lot of people who came to the quay to see him off.

He was invited to talk at the International Pen Club Meeting in London but spent the rest of the journey casually, accompanied by his youngest daughter. He visited his younger son Tomojiro in Paris, where he was studying music. Kyoshi had an informal gathering with various French haikai poets to give a talk on haiku.

While on this journey, Kyoshi emphasizes in his essay that he wanted to make this trip with, "everyday casualness." We should not forget, however, the mettle and spirit he shows in the last five syllables of this haiku. *Kashimadachi* means both the departure of ordinary trips and the special departure of the warriors to the battles in the old days.

Therefore, with this expression, *kashimadachi,* we can sense his spirit and pride in introducing haiku, Japanese original poetry, to European literary society.

No. 39

たとふれば独楽のはぢける如くなり

Tatoureba koma no hajikeru gotoku nari

Literal translation:

Like two spinning tops
We burst away
At the slightest touch

Seasonal word: *koma*, a top (New Year)

This haiku was written in 1937, when Kyoshi was 63 years old.

This is Kyoshi's memorial haiku dedicated to Kawahigashi Hekigotou who passed away on February 1, 1937. In his preface, Kyoshi wrote that he had been good friends with Hekigotou and they often had disputes about haiku. The seasonal word "top" was indeed best chosen to tell us what Kyoshi would have liked to say.

Both of these two famous haiku poets entered Iyo Middle high school in 1888 in Matsuyama. Kyoshi was introduced to his mentor, Shiki, by Hekigotou. After Shiki passed away, Hekigotou took over his post as haiku *senja* (selector) for the newspaper Nihon, and Kyoshi took over as editor-in-chief of the haiku monthly magazine <u>Hototogisu</u>. Although they often fought because of their differing beliefs about haiku, their friendship endured throughout their lives.

They were just like two spinning tops, attracting and coming closer to each other but sharply repelling as soon as they touched.

No. 40

金の輪の春の眠りにはひりけり

Kin no wa no haru no nemuri ni hairikeri

Literal translation:

I have entered
The golden circle of
Spring slumber

Seasonal word: spring slumber, *shunmin, haru no nemuri*

Written in 1942, when Kyoshi was 69 years old.

The image we receive from "the golden circle" must be the sun. It is indeed a very fitting metaphor for the golden sunlight.

But there is more than that. I think this haiku hides something very significant in its depth. Every time I read it, I cannot help having the image of death—not a sad or dismal death, but a happy, contented one that is willingly and thankfully embraced. I think this is because the expression "the golden circle" reminds me of a halo.

In bright, warm sunlight, we fall into a blessed slumber. This is the essential quality of the seasonal word "spring slumber" *shunmin.*

Around 1947, Kyoshi started to develop his theory that haiku is the literature of paradise. However, I can see the budding of this idea as early as this haiku.

No. 41

夏潮の今退く平家亡ぶ時も

Natsushio no ima hiku heike horobu toki mo

Literal translation:

The summer tide is
Ebbing now just like when
Heike-clan was ruined

On June 1st, 1941, Kyoshi was looking over the famous Straits of Hayatomo of Kan-Mon Channel. On the other side of the straits is the Dan-no-Ura, where stands the Akama shrine dedicated to Emperor Antoku, the last infant emperor of the Heike-clan.

Just then, in front of him, the tide suddenly reversed its flow. Looking at this grand ebbing tide, Kyoshi could not help thinking of the battle of Dan-no-Ura, the last war fought between the Heike and Genji clans at this strait back in 1185.

At the beginning of that war, the battle was in Heike's favor, but when the tide reversed, Genji took advantage of the current and defeated Heike, who sank to a watery grave.

The tone of the first half of this haiku is strong and quick, whereas the second half is quiet and melancholy. Both past and present are effectively contrasted and fused in one haiku, leaving lingering echoes in the reader's soul.

No. 42

夏潮を蹴つて戻りて陸に立つ

Natsushio o kette modorite kuga ni tatsu

Literal translation:

I've plowed through the summer tide;
I've returned to my homeland
And stand on the land again

Seasonal word: summer tide

Written on June 11, 1936, when Kyoshi was 63 years old.

In 1936, Kyoshi was invited to the assembly of International Pen Club to give a talk on Haiku. (#38) After traveling around Europe for one month, it took him about forty days on the Hakone-maru, to return to Japan.

After passing through the nostalgic scene of the Inland Sea, the ship anchored at Kobe, which was a special town for Kyoshi. It was in this city where he took care of his mentor, Shiki, who was sick in bed with tuberculosis. Moreover, his son's family was living in Ashiya, the neighboring town. Kyoshi must have felt relieved to come back to Kobe after his long voyage.

The delight bursting through the words of this haiku is almost palpable. This is especially evidenced by his use of three verbs in sequence. The expression "plowing through the summer tide" is also unique. It is the ship that plows through the tide, but we imagine Kyoshi himself battling the tide to return home.

No. 43

籐椅子にあれば草木花鳥来

Touisu ni areba soumoku kachou rai

Literal translation:

Sitting on rattan chair
Trees, weeds, flowers and birds are
Coming to me

Seasonal word: a rattan chair, *touisu* (summer)

Written in 1936, when Kyoshi was 63 years old.

This haiku was composed at a party at the official residence to celebrate Fuhsei, one of his best disciples, who was named as vice-minister of posts and telecommunications. The other haiku written at the same occasion goes as follows; Summer trees and / Summer plants are / Moving towards me.

Aside from birds, what does it mean that trees and plants move towards him? Kyoshi does not like to use personification by nature, so he must be describing what he actually saw.

In his essay written in 1952, Kyoshi wrote about his view on "subjective description and objective description" as follows:

> When we look at flowers and birds with our heart, they become familiar with it, melt into it, and they start to move just as our heart moves and they feel as we feel. In this situation, if we describe what color they are or how they really look, it also describes what we feel in our heart."

And with one more step, it comes back to an objective description again. Thus, the two descriptions make a spiral movement in something of a harmonic fusion.

Another example: "Mosquito-larvae/ Float and sink/ As we like."

How can we understand this piece if we don't understand his interpretation above? Kyoshi's haiku at the beginning of this article is a poem about exactly what he saw and felt.

No. 44

帚木に影といふものありにけり

Hahakigi ni kage to yuu mono arinikeri

Literal translation:

A broom grass casts
What one might call
Its shadow

Seasonal word: *hahakigi*, a broom grass (summer)

Hahakigi, or broom grass, is teardrop-shaped, but its outline cannot be drawn clearly. This indistinct outline of the grass gives vagueness to its existence.

If we look not at the outward shape but inside, at the stems and leaves themselves, we find the stems to be rather thick and pinkish and the leaves frail and pale green. The plant also has a hollow or transparent quality, as we can clearly see through it to the other side. Its colors are unique. Its shape and volume convey both richness and a solemn emptiness.

Kyoshi found the shadow of the grass on the ground to be dark and black with a clear outline of the total shape of the grass. He thought the shadow was much more realistic than the grass itself. Thus, he was more impressed by the real image of the shadow than the indistinctive image of the grass.

No. 45

もの言ひて露けき夜と覚えたり

Mono iite tsuyukeki yoru to oboe-tari

Literal translation:

Uttering something
I sensed it was
A dewy night

Seasonal word: dewy, *tsuyukesi* (autumn)

Written on August 26, 1930, when Kyoshi was 57 years old.

When we read this haiku, we instantly feel that Kyoshi is sitting in a very quiet room. He uttered some words, which broke the entire stillness of the room. When the silence returned, Kyoshi sensed the indication of a dewy night in the echo of his own voice and in the tranquil air of the room.

The word "dewy" has two meanings: one is "full of dew" and the other is "in tears." Therefore, I think a dewy night also means a lonely night.

Three days after this haiku was written, Kyoshi's beloved younger son left for Paris to study music. The phrase "a dewy night" was likely a reflection of his lonely state of mind. We can sympathize with his feelings of deep solitude.

No. 46

肌寒も残る寒さも身一つ

Hada-samu mo nokoru samusa mo mi hitotsu

Literal translation:

From not only chill
But from lingering cold
Nothing else to protect you

Seasonal word: chill, *hadasamu*, (autumn), lingering cold, *nokoru-samusa* (early spring)

Written in October, 1938, when Kyoshi was 64 years old.

Kyoshi visited Staff Sergeant Hukagawa Shoichirou, one of his loyal followers, at the army division of Zentsuji in Shikoku. Shoichirou received a draft into the army in 1937 and had been stationed at Shikoku. His wife was staying near the site with their daughter.

Late in autumn, it was chilly (felt on skin). Kyoshi had a good meeting with him and asked him to take good care of himself in these uncomfortable circumstances.

You may have noticed that there are two seasonal words in this haiku, which indicate different seasons. While this is very unusual and almost forbidden in haiku, in this case, it worked effectively to show the duration of time from October to February and the change of seasons from late autumn to early spring.

We can interpret the meaning of this haiku as follows: this cold season will last for a long time from now till the early spring, when you may still feel lingering cold. In these barracks you may not be able to wear warm clothes to keep your body comfortable. Please take good care of yourself.

No. 47

天地の間にほろと時雨かな

Ametsuchi no awai ni horo to shigure kana

Literal translation:

In the space between
The sky and the earth, delicately and softly
Falls light winter shower

Seasonal word: *shigure*, light winter shower(winter)

Written in 1942, when Kyoshi was 67 years old.

This haiku was written to mourn the death of Suzuki Hanamino, who is responsible for what is called "the era of Hanamino" in the history of <u>Hototogisu</u> at the end of Taisho period.

Hanamino lost his only son, which robbed him of his physical and mental strength. He passed away on 6th of November, 1942. November of the solar calendar is supposed to be October of the lunar calendar and used to be called *shigure-zuki* (the month of light winter shower) when we often have soft winter shower.

In Japanese literature *shigure* is understood to be a symbol of something ephemeral, as it rains and shines unpredictably at this time. The image of a winter shower correlates with the evanescence of our human life. This haiku also gives us the image associated with teardrops.

It was Kyoshi who succeeded in adding a sense of fondness and affection to the otherwise cold and melancholy image of *shigure*.

No. 48

惨として驕らざるこの寒牡丹

San to shite ogorazaru kono kan-botan

Literal translation:

Tragic and heart-rending,
And without haughtiness –
This winter peony before me

Seasonal word: *kan-botan*, a winter-peony

This haiku was created in 1941 when Kyoshi was 66 years old.

It was one of three haiku dedicated at the Memorial meeting for the seventh anniversary of the death of Matsumoto Nagashi, the famous Noh player and haiku poet.

A winter peony, unlike that of early summer, looks solemn amidst the cold in the shade of straw matting. It displays a heartrending, tragic quality that is far from haughtiness.

This image of a winter peony reminds us that Nagashi was famous for his perfect performance of stillness in Noh. What is called *iguse* in Noh is supposed to be the most difficult and severe form of acting—a form that requires perfect stillness in the centre of the stage, without chanting or dancing but nevertheless achieving physical and mental fulfillment. This is indeed the image of the winter peony.

No. 49

旗のごとなびく冬日をふと見たり

Hata no goto nabiku fuyubi o futo mitari

Literal translation:

For a moment I saw
Winter sun light waves
Like a banner

Seasonal word: the winter sun, *fuyubi*

Written in 1938, when Kyoshi was 64 years old.

Unlike the summer sun, which blazes dazzlingly, the heat and light of the winter sun are dim and dull. We long for it and miss it dearly.

In this haiku he says that he saw the winter sun suddenly glare, as if it had spread its wings, and wave like a banner.

In his essay entitled "The Winter Sun," Kyoshi writes about this haiku as follows: I was standing in my garden. There was a little and tight winter sun in the firmament. No wind. No sound. No bird flying. No one there but me. On turning my head, I saw the little winter sun spread its radiance like a flag and wave in a corner of the heaven. It was a great beautiful cloud of light fluttering like a banner."

He also writes that it is a sublime response to his salutations, the human being communicating with the powerful natural force, the winter sun.

No. 50

実朝忌由井の浪音今も高し

Sanetomo-ki yui no namioto ima mo takashi

Literal translation:

Waves at Yui Beach roar
With such might even now
Memorial day of Sanetomo

Seasonal word: Memorial day of Sanetomo, January 29th

Minamoto-no-Sanetomo was the third Shogun of Kamakura Shogunate and prominent in both martial and literal arts. He was assassinated by his nephew at the age of 27.

Kyoshi was sixty-five years old when he wrote this haiku.He was standing at Yui-ga-hama (Yui Beach) listening to the sound of the rough waves and thinking that Sanetomo, too, must have been here listening to the waves eight hundred years ago.

The basic meaning of this haiku is so simple it can be easily understood. The hidden meaning, however, is much more profound and we must pay attention to the poem's implicit clues to understand it.

It is a well known fact that haiku has only seventeen syllables, so it is almost impossible for a poet to express what he wants to say with mere logical explanations. Then what can be done? We must use images or metaphors. We borrow the power from useful, well-chosen words to conjure images and to convey associations in the poem.

Seasonal words are most efficient words for that purpose. If the haiku includes yet another compelling word or metaphor, it will be even more effective. In this haiku, it is *yui-no-namioto*, the sound of waves at Yui beach. It invites readers to associate his unrealized dream of Sanetomo to visit China (Sou) with his most famous poem in his *waka* anthology, *Kinkai-Waka-Shu*. The phrase "even now" links it to the present time. In this way, the evanescence and emptiness of human life is shown in comparison to nature.

No. 51

風多き小諸の春は住み憂かり

Kaze ooki komoro no haru wa sumi ukari

Literal translation:

To live in the spring
Of Komoro's harsh winds –
Gloomy, indeed

Seasonal word: spring

Written at Komoro in March, 1945 when Kyoshi was 71 years old.

Kyoshi moved to Komoro during the war on September 4th, 1944 and stayed there till October 25th, 1947, after the war had ended. This haiku was written right after the first winter he spent there. He expresses his honest feelings about living in this place in March, when it was spring on the calendar yet still windy and cold.

Kyoshi, who was born in Matsuyama, a southern town in Shikoku, was sensitive to the cold. For a man in his seventies, the cold he experienced there for the first time must have been severe.

It was remarkable of Kyoshi to describe the weather of that season there in one phrase "windy spring of Komoro." The exquisite point of this haiku, however, is the expression "gloomy," which is neither "unhappy" nor "miserable."

No. 52

初蝶来何色と問ふ黄と答ふ

Hatsu-chou ku nani iro to tou ki to kotau

Literal translation:

A first butterfly flying;
What color, someone asks –
Yellow, I answer –

Seasonal Word: *hatsu-chou*, a first butterfly, (early spring)

Written at Komoro on March 29, 1946, when Kyoshi was 73 years old.

Kyoshi writes, "It was an unusually warm day. I happened to see a butterfly fly into my garden on a soft breeze."

We can easily imagine how joyful Kyoshi and the guests were to see the first butterfly in early spring. It was a welcome symbol of the arrival of spring in that mountainous village after a long, severe winter.

Haiku is poetry with monologue, but it was more strongly characterized by Shiki when he established haiku out of *renku*. Renku, the mother of haiku, is the only poem with dialogue in the world. When Shiki removed the characteristic of dialogue from haiku, Kyoshi seemed unhappy about it.

Haiku's greetings and salutations ask and address people and other living things. Kyoshi says that haiku is the poem of asking, *sonmon-no-shi*. In this haiku, Kyoshi succeeded in highlighting the importance of dialogue in haiku.

No. 53

兵燹を逃れて山の月の庵

Heisen o nogarete yama no tsuki no io

Literal translation:

Fleeing the fires of
War bombs, we escape
To a moonlit mountain cottage

Seasonal word: the moon (autumn)

Written on May 27th 1945, when Kyoshi was 70 years old.

In May 1945, World War was coming to an end. In March, Tokyo was at-
tacked by an air raid and many other cities and towns all over Japan were
reduced to ashes one by one. Many people living in the capital moved to the
countryside, and many Noh-players moved to Shinshu, where Kyoshi had
been living for a year. Kyoshi happened to meet those Noh-players and other
good friends there, and Komoro came to be dearer to him.

Remember, this haiku was written on May 27th. The moon is a seasonal
word of autumn. While it is possible that they were looking at the moon
that night, it is more likely that Kyoshi thought there was no more suitable
seasonal word than "moon" to describe the happiness and pleasure of the
reunion with his old friends.

No. 54

生かなし晩涼に座し居眠れる

Sei kanashi banryoh ni zashi inemureru

Literal translation:

I doze off
Sitting in the evening cool
How sad and dear is life

Seasonal word: *banryoh*, the evening cool (autumn)

Written on June 8th, 1947. Kyoshi was 72 years old.

While enjoying the cool of the evening in a Japanese room in a friend's mountain villa, seventy-two-year-old Kyoshi dozed off in spite of himself. When he awoke, he was embarrassed for falling asleep and being impolite to his host. Above all, however, he truly felt the sorrow of old age, expressing it as "life is sad."

This meaning is readily apparent even from a superficial reading of this haiku, but I think this simplicity is deceptive because of the word *kanashi*. There are three main meanings for the Japanese *kanashi*: sad (悲し), touching and pathetic (哀し) and dear and beloved (愛し). This *kanashi* used in the above haiku by Kyoshi implies all three meanings simultaneously.

Kyoshi sighs about his old age and diminishing faculties, but he accepts it. He accepts life as it is.

No. 55

人の世も斯く美しと虹の立つ

Hito no yo mo kaku utsukushi to niji no tatsu

Literal translation:

A rainbow rises
Revealing the heavenly beauty
Of our human world

Seasonal word: *niji*, rainbow (summer)

Written on July 18th, 1946 when Kyoshi was 71.

In June, 1946, the celebration of the six-hundredth volume of <u>Hototogisu</u> was held in Komoro. Among the hundred haiku poets present were Aiko and Hakusui, the heroine and hero of Kyoshi's novel "The Rainbow,"

Hakusui was a forlorn young man who was sick in bed with tuberculosis in a hospital in Kamakura. Aiko was also a tubercular patient at the same hospital. They got acquainted with each other and Aiko started to study haiku with him. They fell in love but decided not to get married because of their disease. They lived together with her mother in the countryside

Kyoshi's story "The Rainbow" is about Aiko. When Kyoshi and Aiko were gazing at a rainbow one day, she muttered that she would walk over the rainbow some day to Kamakura to see Kyoshi. He told her that she should cross the rainbow with a walking cane. She answered that she would. Ever since that day, rainbows remind him of Aiko.

With this haiku, Kyoshi wanted to praise Aiko's purity of heart and also the kind affections of the haiku poets around her.

No. 56

敵といふもの今は無し秋の月

Teki to yuu mono ima wa nashi aki no tsuki

Literal translation:

What we call enemies
There are now none;
Autumnal moon

Seasonal word: moon (autumn)

Written on August 22nd, 1945, when Kyoshi was 70 years old.

In his own preface, Kyoshi wrote: "After I listened to the Emperor's Proclamation of the end of the War, I wrote this haiku at the request of the Asahi Newspaper."

When the war was over, Kyoshi was still living in Komoro. He wrote about that day and that haiku in his autobiography as follows:

> When I listened to the Emperor's declaration of the end of the war, I was suffering from a disease like dysentery. As I looked at the Japan Alps from my garden some days before, I wondered what would happen to our beautiful mountains and rivers if we were defeated in this war. Therefore, as soon as I heard the Emperor's declaration of our defeat, this haiku came into my mind.

There is no expression of sorrow, lament, or grief; his belief in haiku was far beyond those emotions. We Japanese have been living with nature ever since the *Mannyo* era, appreciating all its great changes.

When Kyoshi was asked by the newspaper and magazine people what kind of influence the war had on haiku and how haiku might change thereafter, he answered, "As far as haiku is concerned, there is no change at all. We will pursue the same road of haiku."

No. 57

更級や姨捨山の月ぞこれ

Sarashina ya Obasute-yama no tsuki zo kore

Literal translation:

Here it is –
The moon, in Sarashina,
Above Mt.Obasute!

Seasonal word: the moon (autumn)

This haiku was written on September 22nd, 1945, when Kyoshi was 70 years old.

At the beginning of August Kyoshi received the invitation to the meeting at Obasute-yama to see the August full moon of the lunar calendar. This haiku was written on September 22nd, at that gathering.

We have to remember that between the day that Kyoshi accepted the invitation and the day of the gathering, World War ended. Everybody must have gathered there to see the August full moon of Mt. Obasute with all kinds of feelings and thoughts in their minds. The place for the meeting was on the second floor of a farmhouse. "A very suitable countrified lodging," Kyoshi wrote. He also wrote that present among them were a mother whose son had been killed in the South Seas during the War, a man who recently lost his beloved wife, some who had been evacuated by the war, and others who had been in bed in hospitals. All had gathered together to admire the moon in Sarasina at Mt. Obasute.

Mt. Obasute is famous as a place for deserting old people so they can die by themselves and for admiring the moon. "Obasute," one of the masterpieces of Noh-play by Zeami, is written about this theme. Kyoshi must have been thinking about this Noh-play. In the Noh, the abandoned old lady who is playing the leading part solely praises the beautiful moon and wishes to be purified and sublimated by the light of the moon. She would neither complain about her being left in the mountain nor confess her agony about starving to death. Likewise, the people who gathered at Mt. Obasute with Kyoshi did not discuss their unhappy experiences during the war but rather appreciated and admired the clear moonlight.It was not necessary for Kyoshi to tell us how bright and excellent the moon was that night. It was enough to say, "This is –/ The moon of Mt. Obasute"

No. 58

爛々と昼の星見え菌生え

Ranran to hiru no hoshi mie kinoko hae

Literal translation:

In the daylight
Stars are glowing;
Mushrooms are growing

Seasonal word: mushroom, *kinoko*, (autumn)

Written on October 14th, in 1945, when Kyoshi was 72.

This is one of Kyoshi's most famous haiku. While it charms readers with its mysterious power, it also defies easy interpretation.

In October 1945, when Kyoshi was leaving Komoro in Shinano after he had lived there for three years, a lot of haiku poets visited him to say goodbye. At the farewell haiku meeting, one of the poets mentioned that he had seen in the daylight a star's reflection on the water surface at the bottom of a deep well. He also said that he could see some fungi growing on the stone-piled wall of the well.

Upon hearing this story, Kyoshi must have been inspired to create a unique universe in his own mind, one where stars glow in the sky, even in the day-time, and primitive fungi flourish down on the earth. He wanted to say that this universe represents the province of Shinano. This must have been his farewell message of appreciation and thanks for his three-year stay in this unique village.

No. 59

深秋といふことのあり人も亦

Shinshu to yuu koto no ari hito mo mata

Literal translation:

So is there
Something called deepening autumn
In human life

Seasonal word: deepening autumn

Written on October 27th, 1945 when Kyoshi was 71.

When I was young I thought that, among the thousands of haiku written by Kyoshi, this haiku was one of the most difficult to understand. Nowadays, however, I love it very much, as I realize that in human life and human character there is indeed what we might call "deepening autumn."

"Deepening autumn" is the seasonal expression for the solemn feeling permeating nature in the late autumn. Let's think about what nature looks like in Japan in October. The sky is as blue as blue can be after the very hot and humid summer. Hills and fields are colored by autumn leaves, and the air is cool and clear. It is the rich and fruitful time of the harvest. However, it is also the time when symptoms of withering and decline take hold throughout nature.

Soon a struggle will commence between light and shadow. Slowly but steadily the balance between light and shadow will be reversed. It will get cooler, the harvest time will end, and leaves will wither and die.

In short, "deepening autumn" can be understood as a precious time to appreciate balance in nature between light and shadow, growth and decline, in the cycle of the seasons.

When Kyoshi says that "deepening autumn" can be applied to human beings, he is referring to the calm state of mind of a rather elderly person who has lived a spiritual, rich, fulfilling life—that is, a state of mind covering the range of human sentiments: sweet or bitter, pure or impure, light or heavy—which he feels in the depths of his heart.

No. 60

父を恋ふ心小春の日に似たる

Chichi o kou kokoro koharu no hi ni nitaru

Literal translation:

My heart missing my father is
Something like warm sun
On 'little spring' in early winter

Seasonal word: *koharu*, little spring (early winter)

Written on November 18th, 1946, when Kyoshi was 72.

Kyoshi's father, Ike-no-uchi Masatada, used to be a warrior. But when Kyoshi became old enough to recognize him, his father was a farmer who plowed his rice field. After several years he failed in farming and lived the rest of his life quietly and peacefully copying with his handwriting the textbooks of Noh plays.

Literal translation of *koharu* is "a little spring," which means "a warm sunny day like spring in an early winter."

This haiku was written on Kyoshi's little journey to visit the places in northern Kyushu where his father formerly visited—a sentimental journey for his father. During this trip, Kyoshi wrote several haiku, including this one. Most of them are very emotional, which is unusual for him.

On a sunny, warm day, Kyoshi is thinking of his beloved father and his love for a peaceful, lonely day "of a little spring." This very unique metaphor has given immortality to this haiku.

No. 61

去年今年貫く棒の如きもの

Kozo-kotoshi tsuranuku boh no gotoki mono

Literal translation:

Old year, new year –
Just like boh
Carrying through

Seasonal phrase: old year, new year, *kozo-kotoshi* (New Year)

Written on December 20th, 1950 when Kyoshi was 62 years old.

We say "last year" and "this year" when we try to punctuate time. However, time is something like *boh* that we cannot sever, Kyoshi says. He expounded on what "time" is comparing it to *boh* (rhymes with 'sew').

[Translator's notes. What is *boh* in English? I have considered several English approximations of it but have not found an appropriate equivalent. *Boh* is quite an ordinary, everyday word we use in our daily life for any straight piece of wood of any length. It may be likened to a stick, rod, pole, piece of wood, whatever you like, but *boh* in this haiku represents the essence of all.]

Of course, this is something Zen-like. It is practical understanding backed up by Kyoshi's personal experiences. In his *son-mon* he talks with a flower, enters the flower and is assimilated with it. When he watches stars, he goes westward with the stars. If the wind blows, he is blown with the wind and becomes the wind himself. We have come across these experiences in Kyoshi's haiku. In this haiku, Kyoshi might have assimilated into "time."

Now, why is *boh* used here? Why and how does it have such an unearthly, powerful spirit? Perhaps Kyoshi himself might not have been able to interpret it. I dare say that *boh* is Kyoshi himself.

"Old year, new year" was an old seasonal phrase, but the famous literary critic Yamamoto Kenkichi later wrote that the value of this seasonal phrase was determined by this Kyoshi haiku.

No. 62

造化又赤を好むや赤椿

Zouka mata aka o konomu ya aka-tsubaki

Literal translation:

Does the Creator,
As I do, like crimson—
Red camellia

Seasonal word: camellia, *tsubaki* (spring)

Written on February 11, 1948, when Kyoshi was 74 years old.

Along with this haiku, Kyoshi wrote three other haiku about camellia over a two-day period. He loved camellias and wrote of them in a great many haiku throughout his life, most of which are excellent depictions of the flower. However, this haiku and three others are a little different from his earlier ones.

Kyoshi had a strong tendency toward animism. After having spent three years in Komoro, he seemed to converse more easily with nature and to identify with what he was seeing. Therefore, what he saw in camellias at that time must have been the flow of the camellia's life energy. In one of these haiku, he described it as sensual. This sensuality is what is called "Eros"– that is, the soul of the universe.

Kyoshi asks if the Creator, too, loves red just as he does. It seems that Kyoshi has begun to identify with the Creator.

No. 63

海女とても陸こそよけれ桃の花

Ama totemo kuga koso yokere momo-no-hana

Literal translation:

Even women divers
Must be happier on land;
Peach blossoms

Seasonal word: peach blossom, *momo-no-hana* (spring)

This haiku was written on April 8th, 1948, when Kyoshi was 70 years old.

Kyoshi was on the tour to visit Ise-Shima district and had a close-up look at famous women divers working at the outer sea.

The meaning of this haiku is as follows: women divers are gathering and chattering happily after they have worked hard in the sea. Peach blossoms are blooming all around them. Kyoshi thinks that the divers are happier on land than in the sea.

Why are we so charmed by this haiku? Firstly, because the seasonal word "peach blossom" works splendidly in this situation. Peach blossoms are lovely, but earthy and unassuming.

They are a fitting background for a group of young women-divers chatting pleasantly in the sun. I say "young," even though there is no mention of their age in Kyoshi's essay. This description was naturally drawn from the "peach blossoms."

Secondly, in this haiku we sense Kyoshi's warm compassion for these young women-divers whose work in the sea is as demanding as it is dangerous. As in the previous haiku about camellia, we also feel the flow of "Eros."

No. 64

何よりもとり戻したる花明り

Nani yori mo tori-modoshitaru hana-akari

Literal translation:

You have been restored to
Light of cherry blossoms –
To say nothing of everything else

Seasonal word: *hana-akari*, light of cherry blossoms

Written on April 13th, 1949, when Kyoshi was 76 years old.

This is the condolences haiku for blind haiku poet Adsumi Sogan, in Wadayama.

Kyoshi wrote as follows in his famous story "The Story of Little Camellia": Sogan was not born blind. He suddenly lost sight when he was studying at the university during the time of cherry blossoms. The blossoms had just started to fall and their white petals were flickering at the edge of his sight. Then a black curtain slowly descended in his sight until it reached the bottom. White images of the falling petals disappeared. Since then, he could tell darkness from light but was not able to recognize what he saw.

Sogan wrote a lot of great haiku in spite of his blindness. However, this was during the days of confusion after World War and he endured many difficult problems, which troubled him greatly. Grieving over his incapability, he finally lost his entire sight and began to lose even his hearing and appetite. One evening he went upstairs to sleep and was found dead in the morning.

This haiku was dedicated to him. Kyoshi also wrote in the story as follows: Sogan, who lost his eyesight while looking at falling cherry blossoms, must have been reborn in a free space and resumed his clear sight.

How happy Sogan's family must have been that this haiku was a dedication to Adsumi.

No. 65

卯の花のいぶせき門と答へけり

U-no-hana no ibuseki mon to kotae-keri

Literal translation:

At the shabby gate
Covered with white wild flowers –
This was his answer.

Seasonal word: *u-no-hana*, white little flowers of deutzia (early summer)

This haiku was written on May 24th, 1946 at a <u>Hototogisu</u> meeting in Komoro, when Kyoshi was 73 years old.

Kyoshi asked how he could find the location of the next day's haiku meeting, and the person answered, "Please visit the shabby gate which is covered with white deutzia flowers."

U-no-hana, the flower of deutzia, is a symbolic flower of May. Hanging branches of many little white flowers blooming one after another is also the symbol of the coming of summer. On the other hand, we call a long spell of rainy weather *u-no-hana kutashi*, or "rain rotting *u-no-hana*."

Kyoshi wanted to praise everything as it is—that is, to sing of the beauty of beautiful things and the ugliness of ugly things. For Kyoshi there was no difference in value between the beauty and the ugliness. This is the philosophy he practiced after he had conversed with nature in Komoro.

In Komoro, Kyoshi had to endure a hard life at the end of the war. It was very cold and the environment was harsh. He learned of the deaths of many of his friends and acquaintances, one after another. He also worried about his family's future. Through these difficult experiences, he formed his philosophy of acknowledging all beings as they are.

No. 66

明易や花鳥諷詠南無阿弥陀

Akeyasu ya kachoh-fuh-ei namu-amida

Literal translation:

Dawn breaking early
Kachoh-fuh-ei
Namuamida

Seasonal word: dawn breaking early, *akeyasushi*, (summer)

This haiku was written on July 19th 1954, when Kyoshi was 81 years old.

Kyoshi went to Kanoh-san Jinya-ji in Chiba prefecture on July 13th, and stayed there for a week. This is one of the seven haiku he wrote on the last day.

Kachoh-fuh-ei is the unique theme Kyoshi developed and articulated throughout his life. He believed that haiku was poetry that sang about everything in nature, including but not limited to the birds and flowers.

To understand this haiku, we must have the fundamental knowledge of *namuamida*. *Namu* is Sanskrit for "to worship" or "to take refuge in the Buddha wholeheartedly." *Amida* stands for *amida-butsu*, the Buddha of the Infinite Light and Life who presides over the Pure Land of Highest Joy, *gokuraku-johdo*. Therefore, *namu-amidabutsu* may be interpreted, as "I worship the Buddha of the Infinite Light who presides over the Pure Land of Highest Joy."

For the Johdo sect, *namu-amida* holds great, profound meaning. It is called *nenbutsu* to chant it. With this, *nenbutsu* people are promised passage to *gokuraku-johdo*, the pure land of highest joy. In the Johdo sect, *namu-amidabutsu* is the most sacred, important word of the doctrine, the method of religious acts or deeds taking one to the final goal, and also so-called "gospel."

Now, look at the haiku once again with this knowledge. Kyoshi says that in the endlessness of eternity, we are living only for our religion as ephemeral beings with a brief lifespan. Kyoshi believes in *kachoh-fuh-ei* as well as in *namu-amida*, and wants to save us and redeem us, who are ephemeral and mortal, that is, *akeyasui*.

Now we understand that *kachoh-fuh-ei*, like *namu-amidabutsu, reaches* beyond explanation of haiku's fundamental meaning. It has become the doctrine, the method of religious austerities and gospel of *gokuraku-no-bungaku*, a literature of paradise.

No. 67

虚子一人銀河と共に西へ行く

Kyoshi hitori ginga to tomo ni nishi e yuku

Literal translation:

Kyoshi alone
Along with the Milky Way
Goes to the west

Seasonal word: *ginga*, the Milky Way (summer)

Written on July 23rd, 1949, when Kyoshi was 74 years old.

In his preface, he writes: "At midnight, I got out of the mosquito net, opened the wooden sliding door, and looked up toward the Milky Way." He did not just look at the sky, but "looked up toward the Milky Way."

On this occasion, Kyoshi wrote five haiku, including the one above. The other four are as follows:

(1) 銀河中天老の力をそれに得つ   Ginga chuhten oi no chikara o sore ni etsu

> From the Milky Way
> Up in the heavens, I the aged
> Receive the power

(2) 銀河西へ人は東へ流れ星   Ginga nishi e hito wa higashi e nagareboshi

> Milky Way to the West,
> Human beings to the East;
> Shooting star

(3) 西方の浄土は銀河落るところ   Saihoh no johdo wa ginga otsuru tokoro

> The Pure Land
> Of the West is where
> The Milky Way falls

(4) なつかしの戸締める隣月更けて　*Natsukashi no to shimeru tonari tsuki fukete*

> Nostalgic sound of
> Neighbor's sliding door;
> Moon of deepening night

We will not be able to understand the theme of these haiku if we don't recognize that this series sings of the earth's rotation. The earth turns around every day from west to east on its own axis. Naturally, the sky moves westward, if seen from the earth, and all beings, including man, move eastward. Kyoshi is feeling and sensing the rotation of the earth.

The poet is so deeply fascinated by the magnificence and grandeur of the Milky Way that it overtakes him. We may call this a kind of mystic experience. This sort of mysticism is noticeable in many of Kyoshi's haiku. Then he is led to the idea of "the Pure Land in the West" (3). This image tells us that Kyoshi ponders death on a regular basis. He believes that the Western Paradise lies at the place where the Milky Way falls.

With this in mind, I would like to show you another haiku written by Kyoshi in October of the same year.

> At the end of my life　　わが終り銀河の中に身を投げん
> I shall throw myself
> Into the Milky Way (Waga owari ginga no naka ni mi o nagen)

In haiku (4), however, Kyoshi comes back to reality upon hearing a neighbor's sliding doors. He is left forlorn and filled with nostalgia.

I believe that this haiku is best appreciated when read along with the other four written on the same day.

No. 68

稲稔り蜻蛉つるみ子を背負ひ

Ine minori tomboh tsurumi ko o seoi

Literal translation:

Rice plants ripen
Dragonflies mate
Babies are carried on backs

Seasonal word: *ine*, rice plant, and *tomboh*, dragonfly (autumn)

Written in August 1947, when Kyoshi was 73.

As early as 1912, Kyoshi wrote a literary sketch entitled "The Busy Creator." It was about the products of the creator rather than the Creator Himself.

In 1915, he wrote a haiku as follows;

The Creator has already been
Extremely busy enough;
And yet, we graft trees!

Here in this haiku, Kyoshi assumes that an omnipotent Creator exists and that it takes charge of all creation. However, his image was not yet concrete.

In 1917 Kyoshi wrote another literary sketch entitled "One day in Tokyo", which clearly indicates his deepening view of the Creator. This sketch is written about the day of the Buddhist service for his deceased eldest brother.

Kyoshi writes: "Our deceased brother is saved by Amida Buddha. If our life is just like a flower on a tree, it is only a revelation of the great power of life at its essence. And there at that essence we also expect to find Amida Buddha."

I have often mentioned Kyoshi's animism. In this animism, however, everything in the universe has its own individual soul and spirit. Now Kyoshi concludes that there is Amida Buddha in the essence of every being.

No. 69

月を思ひ人を思ひて須磨にあり

Tsuki o omoi hito o omoite suma ni ari

Literal translation:

Thinking of the moon
Thinking of the person
I am at Suma

Seasonal word: the moon (autumn)

Written on September 14th, 1951, when Kyoshi was 76.

Kyoshi visited the place at Suma where a convalescent home used to be.

His mentor, Shiki, went to China as a war correspondent in 1890. On his way back to Kobe on the warship, he coughed up blood. He was carried straight into Kobe Hospital from the harbor and moved to Suma Rest House where he had a brief recovery. Kyoshi stayed with him the entire time.

Upon Shiki's recovery, Kyoshi headed back to Tokyo. Shiki thanked him for his company and asked him to become his successor in his new haiku innovation.

Thus, Suma had been a special place for Kyoshi, full of memories shared with Shiki.

No doubt, the person Kyoshi is thinking of in this haiku is Shiki. If that person is Shiki, the meaning of the phrase "Thinking of the moon" naturally refers to the moon he looked up at the night Shiki passed away. Readers may recall the famous mourning haiku written by Kyoshi right after Shiki's death (see #17).

Fifty years later, Kyoshi was standing where the old convalescent home used to be, looking at the moon and thinking deeply of Shiki. (Since ancient times, Suma has been a famous place for viewing the moon.) The next day Kyoshi left Kobe by boat for their old hometown, Matsuyama, to attend the Shiki Memorial Day. There he wrote the following haiku:

I crossed the sea / with no moon, to attend / the Memorial Day of Shiki

No. 70

彼一語我一語秋深みかも

Kare ichi-go ware ichi-go aki fukami-kamo

Literal translation:

He utters a word
I utter a word –
Autumn is deepening!

Seasonal word: deep autumn, *shinshuh*

Written in October 1950, when Kyoshi was 75.

After a gathering, Kyoshi and another man were lingering quietly, listening to the sounds of autumn. His companion uttered a simple word or phrase and Kyoshi replied equally simply. With this he sensed that autumn was deepening.

The man may have said, "How quiet", and Kyoshi may have answered, "Indeed." The situation could be imagined in many ways. The reticence of these two people is effective in depicting the quiet atmosphere of autumn.

Kyoshi says that to "sketch" in haiku is to isolate and focus on his own specific subject or detail within the great universe. He calls this the "small universe" of the poet. What Kyoshi calls "nature" is not the metaphysical nature in Western literature but the nature of Oriental civilization. We human beings are a part of nature, as are flowers, birds, or any animate or inanimate beings. The changing of the seasons, transition of flowers, life and death of human beings are all merely elements or phenomena of this great universe.

No. 71

草枯に真赤な汀子なりしかな

Kusakare ni makkana Teiko narishi-kana

Literal translation:

On withering grasses
There stood Teiko
Dressed in her bright red

Seasonal word: *kusakare*, withering grasses, (late autumn)

Kyoshi took me on his trip to Kyuhshuh. It was our second trip together since I had decided to study haiku in earnest. The day after our return, we attended a haiku gathering at the Takarazuka Hotel to meet haiku poets in the Kansai area.

At the hotel, there was a garden and a beautiful lawn, which was crowded with haiku poets. I wanted to be alone, so I hid in the backyard where there was withering grass. There I unexpectedly found Kyoshi standing quietly all by himself. I was going to speak to him, but I stopped approaching him when I sensed I was disturbing his concentration. Kyoshi stood motionless, silently gazing at me. I was dressed in red.

Kyoshi would often tell me that haiku is the literature of reticence. At that time, I learned the invaluable principle that reticence is also required when we create our haiku.

When I read this haiku in the haiku meeting, I could tell in a moment that it was Kyoshi's. Since then, my interpretation of this haiku has changed a little. Kyoshi must have likened my inexperienced enthusiasm for haiku to a fire. Furthermore, he must have been touched to see the flow of life in my youthfulness. In his haiku of camellia (see #62), he admired red camellias because of their strong beautiful flow of life energy. I may not have been pretty, but I was certainly young.

No. 72

地球一万余回転冬日にこにこ

Chikyuh ichiman-yo kaiten fuyuhi nikoniko

Literal translation:

More than ten thousand
Rotations of earth;
Winter sun beams delight

Seasonal word: *fuyuhi*, winter sun

Written in December 1954, when Kyoshi was 81 years old.

This is the haiku Kyoshi wrote to congratulate a couple of famous haiku poets, Dr. Igarashi Bansui and Yaeko, on their thirtieth wedding anniversary. During their thirty years of marriage, the earth had rotated on its axis about ten thousand times. In the first two lines of this haiku, Kyoshi sang about the tremendous number of rotations of the earth. It is a fantastic opening to the poem. The third line leads it to a satisfying ending using seven syllables.

This haiku has more than seventeen syllables. However, there must be many who do not even notice its broken rhythm, or at least are not bothered by it.

I will tell you a secret. It is well known that Kyoshi was well versed in Noh-play. In Noh-chant there is a rhythm to sing two sounds in one simple time. In this rhythm, the last seven syllables can be read in five syllables. Moreover, the first two lines count seven and five syllables respectively, which is exactly the orthodox rhythm of the Noh chant. When Kyoshi started this haiku with a seven-five pattern, the last line was naturally affected by the Noh rhythm, his inner rhythm.

Dr. Igarashi Bansui and Yaeko, to whom this haiku was dedicated, had lived very honorable lives and are loved and respected by many people. They were very famous haiku poets. All through those happy years the sun had been watching them, and, now on their thirtieth anniversary, the sun is smiling happily at them. With his unique phrase "the winter sun beams delight, *huyuhi nikoniko*," Kyoshi pays his highest tribute to them.

No. 73

惟る御生涯や萩の露

Omonmiru on-shougai ya hagi no tsuyu

Literal translation:

Reflecting with deep
Reverence for your life;
Dewdrops on a bush clover

Seasonal word: *tsuyu*, dewdrop (autumn)

Written in February 1953, when Kyoshi was 80 years old.

Hagi is a typical autumn flower in Japan and is called Japanese bush clover.

This haiku was written according to the wishes of Yamaoka Suika. Suika wanted to build a slab stone with Kyoshi's haiku next to the tombstone of Kyoshi's grandfather on his mother's side.

Kyoshi writes in his foreword that his grandfather became a *rohnin* (a masterless *samurai*) when he was young and lived his life out of his fief by teaching at *terakoya* (a private elementary school) for the rest of his life. He was welcomed by the village people and received an honorable burial ceremony there when he passed away.

Generally speaking, Kyoshi thought a great deal about his family and ancestors. When he came to understand the rather unfortunate life of his grandfather, Kyoshi tried hard to find his tomb and paid a respectful visit there at the end of 1938. In light of this, Yamamoto Suika, haiku poet of the village, decided to build a monument of Kyoshi's haiku next to his grandfather's tomb.

The word *omonmiru* is very suitable and thoughtful Japanese for showing his love and reverence for the hardships and challenges of his grandfather's life. "Dewdrops on *hagi*" is also a very effective seasonal phrase for fleeting and transient life.

No. 74

笹鳴が初音となりし頃のこと

Sasanaki ga hatsune to narishi koro no koto

Literal translation:

I remember when
Twittering of nightingales
Grew into their first songs

Seasonal word: *hatsune,* the first song of a nightingale

This haiku has its foreword as follows: "At the memorial party in Matsuyama to celebrate the 600th volume of Hototogisu, I met Yanagihara Kyokudoh who founded the periodical."

The 600th memorial issue of Hototogisu was published in December 1946. In that chaotic aftermath of World War II, a big celebration could not be held in Tokyo. Instead, a series of memorial gatherings were held in various cities around Japan.

In November 1946, the commemoration was held in Matsuyama, where Kyoshi met Yanagihara Kyokudoh who established Hototogisu. Later when Kyoshi was asked to write a memorial haiku for the occasion, he wrote the above haiku in remembrance of that ceremony and Kyokudo.

If one is familiar with the story behind this haiku, it is clear that the twittering of a nightingale implies the establishment of Hototogisu in Matsuyama by Kyokudoh in 1897. "The first song of the nightingale" refers to Kyoshi's re-establishment in Tokyo in October 1898. These are magnificent metaphors.

Another important characteristic of this haiku is the fact that it contains greetings and courtesies from Kyoshi to Kyokudoh. By describing the change of tone of a nightingale, he expresses his message that any great change in our life is nothing but one of many phenomena in nature.

No. 75

ゆらぎ見ゆ百の椿が三百に

Yuragi-miyu hyaku no tsubaki ga san-byaku ni

Literal translation:

Swaying and fluttering
One hundred camellias look like
Three hundred

Seasonal word: *tsubaki*, a camellia (spring)

Written in March 1951, when Kyoshi was 77 years old.

The meaning of this haiku is very clear. A hundred camellias swaying and fluttering appear to be as many as three hundred. Of course, these numbers are not the actual numbers. In a sweet tone, the poem describes the scene of a great many camellias flickering and wavering, which must have been the exact view in the eyes of Kyoshi, the great observer.

I recall coming across some allusions to camellias in his "Story of Little Camellia" (Tsubakiko Monogatari). When I studied the Editor's Notes that Kyoshi wrote at the end of each Hototogisu over several months around the time this haiku was written, I discovered that Kyoshi actually had a cerebral condition in those days.

He writes of feeling a little numbness in his tongue and left limb. He also confesses to feeling unpleasant echoes in his brain when he sings Noh-chants. Kyoshi promises that he will take better care of himself. These notes show that Kyoshi had been convalescing at that time.

Now we realize that the great many swaying camellias could have been the symptoms of his dizziness, and that he appreciated the beautiful flickering of the flowers without perceiving his own vertigo.

No. 76

牡丹の日々の衰へ見つゝあり

Bohtan no hibi no otoroe mitsutsuari

Literal translation:

I am watching
The peony declining
Day after day

Seasonal word: *bohtan (botan)*, a peony

Written on April 25th, 1931, when Kyoshi was 77 years old.

The magnificence of a peony cannot last longer than three days. On the first three days, the flower opens early in the morning and closes at night to sleep. Around the fourth day it cannot close anymore, and, slowly weakening, stays open at night. As it ages, the allure of the flower grows. The peony remains lovely and bewitching until the moment it scatters its last petal.

From Kyoshi's expression we learn two unique points. First, by observing the peony closely every day, he realizes that it keeps declining and losing its magnificence. Second, Kyoshi is not saddened by its weakening and withering. He appreciates and admires every second of its change and accepts it as it is.

In the last years of his life, Kyoshi advocated that haiku, when it sang of anything in nature just as did of birds and flowers, would be the language of heaven. He said there was no difference between a human life of eighty-eight years and the short, one-year life of a flower. He believed everything was a manifestation of life in the universe.

No. 77

面脱ぎて嫉妬の汗の美しく

Men nugite shitto no ase no utsukushiku

Literal translation:

The Noh-mask taken off
Perspiration of jealousy
Glistens beautiful

Seasonal word: *ase*, perspiration (summer)

Written on May 25, 1954, when Kyoshi was 80 years old.

In the preface for this haiku, Kyoshi says he wrote this haiku according to Ohan's request for a haiku on '*Aoi-no-ue*'. O-han, Takehara Han, was a famous dancer in the Japanese classical style called '*Jiuta-mai*', a member of the Japan Academy of Art, and a famous haiku poet.

Aoi-no-ue is the name of a lady with whom Genji was madly in love and who was killed by the apparition of his ex-lover, Rokujoh-no-miyasudokoro. Judging from the expression "the mask taken off," this does not refer to the lady herself but to the Noh play called "Aoi-no-ue."

In the Noh play "Aoi-no-ue," the mental and physical fatigue of the *shite* (lead actor) playing the part of Miyasudokoro must have been tremendous. Kyoshi describes the sweat running down the face of the Noh-actor who has just taken off his female demon mask as "beautiful."

One wonders why Kyoshi said the sweat of jealousy is beautiful. Miyasudokoro is jealous of Aoi-no-ue, who has become the legal wife of Genji and is expecting their baby soon. Her jealousy grows stronger and stronger until the spirit of her jealousy escapes from her body while she is sleeping and maliciously haunts Aoi-no-ue lying in her bed during labor. Miyasudokoro doesn't consciously know about it.

One day, however, she recognizes that the scent she smells on herself after she awakens is exactly the same scent a priest is burning by Aoi-no-ue's bedside to protect her from evil spirits. Now she has to face the dark side of her consciousness. Being such a proud lady, she must feel a certain amount of shame and hatred toward herself. In the last scene, her evil spirit is defeated by the religious power. Because of her nobility, intelligence, and pride, Miyasudokoro accepts the truth and defeat of her unconscious spirit. I believe this is why Kyoshi says the perspiration of jealousy is beautiful.

朴散華而して逝きし茅舎はも

Hoh sange shikoushite yukishi Bohsha wamo

Literal translation:

Like a Buddhist rite,
White magnolias scatter –
Bohsha has passed away

Seasonal word: *hoh*, magnolia (summer)

This haiku was written in June 1951, when Kyoshi was 77, lamenting the passing of Bohsha, who had died on July 17th 1941 at the age of 45. Bohsha is one of Kyoshi's most beloved and most famous protégés. It is obvious that this haiku was remembering Bohsha's following masterpiece:

White magnolia fallen
Like a Buddhist rite and
Gone to nowhere

A magnolia was standing outside the window of the room in which Bohsha was bedridden. He watched the white magnolia every day. One day, however, it fell, leaving behind a great emptiness. When that flower died, Bohsha's soul seemed to dissipate, leaving nothing more than his ailing, withered body. Kyoshi understood that Bohsha had lost his will to live. Actually, although it is thought of as his swan-song, this haiku was not composed on Bohsha's deathbed.

On the day of Bohsha's death, Kyoshi wrote his famous haiku of condolence and ten years later wrote this haiku dedicated to Bohsha. Kyoshi remembered Bohsha's death with the deepest love and regret. The impact he received from Bohsha's expression "Hoh sange" (white magnolia scattered / like a Buddhist rite) was very impressive. I believe that this haiku was Kyoshi's *sonmon*—that is, addressing, greeting, and asking for his beloved poet in the other world.

No. 79

すぐ来いといふ子規の夢明易き

Sugu koi to iu Shiki no yume akeyasuki

Literal translation:

"Come soon,"
Said Shiki, in my dream.
Dawn breaks early

Seasonal word: dawn breaks early (summer)

This haiku was written on July 19th 1954, at the fourth haiku meeting of what is called *Keiko-kai* (Kyoshi's training gatherings for college students). He was 80 years old.

About fifty years before, in 1906, Shiki wrote the following famous haiku:
「小夜しぐれ上野を虚子の来つつあらむ」

Light winter shower at night
Kyoshi must be coming now
Around Ueno

Shiki is impatiently waiting for Kyoshi, (thinking he should have arrived in Ueno by now) as he listens to the light rain showers. It is clear that Kyoshi was reminded of this Shiki's haiku when he wrote this.

At the time when Shiki wrote the above haiku, the relationship between him and Kyoshi was rather strained. Shiki was suffering terribly from a chronic disease, spinal caries, and was not able to move without assistance. He tended to rely upon his beloved protégé, Kyoshi, and wanted to train him as his successor. Kyoshi, on the other hand, wanted to free himself from Shiki's restrictions. Moreover, he was in love with a woman named Ito, who was the daughter of his lodging owner.

This friction was totally abated in 1908 when Kyoshi decided to become the publisher of Hototogisu, which was moved from Matsuyama to Tokyo so that Kyoshi could begin his new life with Ito. When asked to help him, Shiki pointed out Kyoshi's weak points and flaws but nevertheless agreed to help Kyoshi. In this way they finally became true comrades and kindred spirits. Since that time, Hototogisu has come to play a leading role in the history of haiku literature.

Given his age, Kyoshi may have been a little tired with four haiku meetings in two days, surrounded by young students. He dreamt of Shiki beckoning him.

No. 80

風生と死の話して涼しさよ

Fuhsei to shi no hanashi shite suzushisa-yo

Literal translation:

Talking of death
With Fuhsei –
Coolness of summer

Seasonal word: cool, coolness (summer)

Written on July 30th 1957, when Kyoshi was 83 years old.

There is a report of an interview with Fuhsei about this haiku.

In the interview, Fuhsei described how this haiku came about.

Fuhsei was chatting with other poets at a haiku gathering. He complained about his neurosis and mentioned that he was afraid of dying. A doctor remarked that Fuhsei must be suffering from a nervous breakdown. Overhearing this, Kyoshi sensei showed his interest and joined their conversation.

Later in the haiku meeting they found the above haiku. Knowing it was written by Kyoshi, some of them selected it. Fuhsei didn't because, Fuhsei said, he did not understand why it was cool to have talked with him about his fear of death. Unfortunately, he did not remember what Kyoshi said during their chat. To gain insight into what Kyoshi might have said to Fuhsei, all we need to do is study Kyoshi's view of life and death in his later years.

Judging from his haiku and essays during those years, Kyoshi seems to be free from any attachment, antagonism, or self- righteousness. His philosophy is that the life and death of human beings is equivalent to the blooming and dying of blossoms. We sense Kyoshi's acknowledgement that our lives just flow through the great, beautiful universe.

If we imagine what Kyoshi might have said to Fuhsei, it would be something like this: we should appreciate our life, but when we die, we should also appreciate our death; we should accept everything as it is.

No. 81

大空の青艶にして流れ星

Ohzora no seien ni shite nagareboshi

Literal translation:

In the heavens,
Grand, vivid and erotic:
A shooting star

Seasonal word: a shooting star, *nagareboshi* (autumn)

Written on September 9th, 1955. Kyoshi was 81.

September is the month that Shiki passed away. From Kyoshi's other haiku of this month, we realize that he wrote these haiku from his deeper feelings about facing "death." Ordinarily, shooting stars are sung as symbolic subjects on which we make wishes. But the shooting star Kyoshi sang of here is different.

In this haiku and other ones composed on the same occasion, the encounter with a shooting star casts various shadows in Kyoshi's mind. He feels not only the reality of the faraway sky at midnight but the uncertainty and strangeness of life. I imagine it is about this time in his life when Kyoshi's world comes in contact with "the other world."

In addition to this haiku, Kyoshi composed about ten others on the subject of shooting stars. These haiku could be called the "banquet of stars in the autumn night." But they are not the only banquet of stars. For Kyoshi, haiku itself was a banquet of all living beings and all phenomena in the universe.

No. 82

暁烏文庫内灘秋の風

Akegarasu bunko uchinada aki no kaze

Literal translation:

Akegarasu Library,
Dunes of Uchinada –
Autumn wind

Seasonal word: autumn wind

This haiku was written on October 4th, 1956, when Kyoshi was 82.

Kyoshi had visited the Akegarasu Library in Kanazawa the previous day. It is the library at Kanazawa University to which Akegarasu Haya, whose haiku name was Himu, donated several thousand of his books. He was a priest of the Shinshuh-Ohtani-sect and began to write haiku when he was a student at the University of the Shinshuh sect of Buddhism. In 1900, he began attending Kyoshi's haiku circle and on occasion gave Kyoshi lectures on religion.

Uchinada is a town in the north of Kanazawa facing the Japan Sea. In 1952, the U.S. Army used the dunes in that town as a firing range. The towns-people fiercely opposed this, marking the beginning of the resistance against the military occupation. Kyoshi visited there in 1956, one year before it was returned to Japan.

In his essay "The Trip in the Age," Kyoshi writes about this haiku as follows:

> The readers may laugh at this haiku, saying they don't understand what it means. I keep this haiku in my mind as a report. Haiku is a report of our life through the four seasons. In 1939, I wrote in the preface of my "Haiku Diary" that spiritual life is a deep tide, while haiku are waves on the surface of our life.

No. 83

我のみの菊日和とはゆめ思はじ

Ware nomi no kiku-biyori towa yume omowaji

Literal translation:

In no way do I imagine
Such fine chrysanthemum weather
Is meant only for me

Seasonal word: *kiku-biyori*, fine chrysanthemum weather (autumn)

Written on November 3rd, 1954 when Kyoshi was 80 years old.

In the preface of this haiku, Kyoshi writes: "I was invited to the Imperial Court to receive the Medal of Cultural Merits, *bunka-kunshoh*."

On November 3rd,1954 Kyoshi had the honor of receiving the Medal of Cultural Merits from the Emperor. He was the first haiku poet to ever receive it. He was showered with blessings and admiration.

From his other haiku, we find that right after he got the notification Kyoshi visited Shiki's tomb to tell him about it. He must have wished that his beloved mentor, Shiki, had been alive to share this honor with him. It is Shiki who felt strongly that haiku should be appreciated as great literature equal to any other genres and who contributed greatly to the advancement of haiku.

On the same day he wrote the above haiku, Kyoshi wrote the following piece:

Chrysanthemum day / Is fading into evening / I am tired

It is easy to imagine how tired Kyoshi must have been at the end of such a long day in the Imperial Court. For him, life and writing haiku were one and the same. The spirit flowing at the bottom of this haiku was the same as the calm and simple stream of life that flowed through the four seasons.

No. 84

わが庭や冬日健康冬木健康

Waga niwa ya fuyuhi kenkou fuyuki kenkou

Literal translation:

My garden –
Healthy is the winter sun
Healthy are the winter trees

Seasonal words: *huyuhi*, the winter sun, and *huyuki*, winter trees.

Written in 1957, when Kyoshi was 83 years old.

'The winter sunlight is usually thought of as weak and faint during winter. Because of its dimness, we often sing of winter sunlight "dropping from behind the clouds" in haiku. Winter trees, as well, are considered frail. In the above haiku, however, Kyoshi says that both the winter sun and the winter trees in his garden look healthy. Through what kind of eyes is old Kyoshi praising the nature of his wintry garden? We would like to understand his view of nature, his view of life.

In my previous essays, I have talked about the animistic view of nature Kyoshi had possessed since he was young. I have also thought about his principle that something like the great power of Amida Buddha exists at the essence of nature. Even if a flower dies, it means another flower is born somewhere else in the universe. While he was living in Komoro, he was always communing and deepening his communication with nature. He eventually came to understand the power of life of this universe.

The winter sun dropping into his garden and the shapes of winter trees are indeed very weak but they represent the reality in the rhythm of the universe, that is to say, they are in good health. This is the positive view of the world Kyoshi attained in the last years of his life.

No. 85

干鮫を喰積の昆布巻にせん

Hoshi-haze o kuidsumi no kobumaki ni sen

Literal translation:

With this dried goby
I will make rolled kelp
For kuidsumi

Seasonal phrase *kuidsumi*: a stack of boxes with various kinds of festive food for the New Year.

Written in 1950, when Kyoshi was 76 years old.

Kyoshi writes in his preface that Zenjidoh sent him some dried gobies he had caught himself.

One of the foods contained in kuidsumi is *Kobumaki*, rolled and seasoned kelp with fish in the middle. Usually herring is used, but here Kyoshi says he will use *haze* (English "goby") sent by Zenjidoh. It sounds delicious, but for Kyoshi it is even more meaningful, as it had given by Zenjidoh.

Yoshioka Zenjidoh used to be a famous follower of Kyoshi. However, when a new wave of haiku began to take hold, he was greatly influenced by it. Finally, in 1935, he declared that he would create and publish "haiku without seasonal words." In 1936, Kyoshi revoked his membership in Hototogisu.

We can easily understand how pleased Kyoshi was when, after fifteen years, Zenjidoh sent him some dried gobies he himself had caught. And you can easily imagine how delighted and grateful Zenjidoh was to receive this haiku from Kyoshi.

No. 86

羽子つこか手鞠つこかともてなしぬ

Hago tsukoka temari tsukoka to motenashinu

Literal translation:

A delight to welcome you, young ladies.
A game of hane-tsuki?
A game of temari?

Seasonal words: hanetsuki, temari (New Year)
Hanetsuki : a typical traditional Japanese game for children and young ladies during New Year holidays, played with a small shuttlecock and a small paddle
Temari: traditional Japanese handball for little girls to play. In old days the ball was handmade by grandmothers with cotton and strings, decorated and embroidered with colorful threads

This haiku was written on February 1st, 1951, when Kyoshi was 77 years old.

In December 1950, Kyoshi had a slight stroke and had to rest. Fortunately, his condition was not very serious. Although he had nearly recovered two weeks later, he found he was getting tired easily, so he began taking better care of himself. In March of that year, the task of selecting haiku from the subscribers of <u>Hototogisu</u> was permanently taken over by his eldest son, Toshio.

This haiku was written during those quiet days after his convalescence. On one of those days, five pretty geisha girls from Shinbashi visited Kyoshi in Kamakura as "New Year visitors in February" *nigatsu-reija*. We can easily imagine how happy and delightful Kyoshi must have been to welcome these pretty young ladies.

As a convalescent, Kyoshi becomes more conscious of his old age and grows fonder of beautiful geisha girls. This is not merely love; it is also the flow of living essence.

On the same day, Kyoshi also wrote four other haiku, which I will introduce here:

◎ *Spring of my humble cottage –*
To receive a visit from
Such beautiful ladies

◎ *Lady-visitors*
In this thatched cottage;
New Year day of the lunar calendar

◎ *All these ladies*
Love accomplishments;
Ume blossoms (Ume is Japanese apricot)

◎ *Please come again next year*
At the time of gathering
Seri, spring herb (Seri is Japanese parsley, one of the seven Japanese herbs for
the New Year.)

Reading these haiku, we can easily imagine how much the poet enjoyed the company of the young geisha girls and how delighted he was to welcome these ladies.

No. 87

闘志尚存して春の風を見る

Tohshi nao sonshite haru no kaze o miru

Literal translation:

Steadfast in my soul,
My fighting spirit remains
And I see the spring breeze

This haiku was written in 1950, when Kyoshi was 76 years old.

Seasonal word: *harukaze*, spring breeze

On reading this haiku, you will think of Kyoshi's famous piece we have already read in the second essay of this series. It goes like this:

On the foothill I stood / Determined and resolute – / Spring breeze (See #2)

It was written in 1913 when he was 39 years old. In brief, Kyoshi determined here to put aside writing novels and return to writing haiku and mentoring haiku poets. This decision was made in defiance of resistance to the movement of haiku led by Hekigotou to ignore the conventions of using seasonal words and seventeen syllables in haiku.

Now in 1950, was there any special reason in the world of haiku that he had to look once again at spring breeze with his fighting spirit? Kyoshi published The Road towards Haiku (Haiku-e-no-Michi) in 1955. In that book he often relates that haiku is the poem to sing of everything in nature just as of flowers and birds (*kachoh-fuh-ei-shi*). He also explains there that this decision seems to have been one of the greatest things he achieved in his life.

We understand Kyoshi's determination has kept burning quietly against those who would destroy the literary tradition of haiku. The spring breeze Kyoshi is now looking at is blowing softly and warmly, full of nourishing energy.

この池の生々流転蝌蚪の紐

Kono ike no seisei- ruten kato no himo

Literal translation:

Circle of life
In this pond —
Cord of tadpole spawn

Seasonal word: tadpole, *kato* (spring)

This haiku was written in 1956 when Kyoshi was 82 years old.

Seisei-ruten means that all beings under the sun keep changing by repeating living and dying, generation after generation.

One day in spring, Kyoshi was standing by a pond where tadpoles were born one after another out of jelly-like eggs wrapped with a type of cord.

Watching these newly hatched tadpoles, Kyoshi thinks about the life activity of frogs, that they maintain their existence by constantly repeating life and death. This pond is the universe for these frogs. And in this universe they have kept up their *seisei-ruten* for a long time. We feel as if Kyoshi were addressing those frogs to sing a song of their praise of life.

Another one of Kyoshi's famous haiku on tadpoles goes like this: The sun has moved / Dark is the water / Of tadpoles. This haiku was written in 1924, when Kyoshi was 50 years old. In that haiku, Kyoshi's focuses only on the surface of the pond; he doesn't look into the water or refer to the past.

In this haiku, however, his inner sight goes back to the past and looks into frogs' life and death over time. This reflects Kyoshi's acceptance of the universe and everything in nature as it is.

No. 89

牡丹の一弁落ちぬ俳諧史

Bohtan no ichi-ben ochinu haikaishi

Literal translation:

Glorious peony
Of haikai's history
Has lost a petal

Seasonal word: *bohtan (botan)*, peony (summer)

This haiku was written on May 13th, 1956, when Kyoshi was 82 years old.

It has a short preface: "Matsumoto Takashi passed away."

Matsumoto Takashi was born in 1906 in Tokyo in the distinguished family of an eminent Noh musician. His father, Matsumoto Nagashi, was a famous master Noh performer. He started practicing Noh dance at the age of six, made his debut at nine, but had to give up his career as a Noh player when he was fifteen due to a medical condition.

His father had been studying haiku under Kyoshi, and Takashi also started writing haiku under Kyoshi's tutelage when he was 15 years old. In 1929, at age 24, he received the honor of the opening haiku *(kantoh)* of Hototogisu. He became one of the magazine's preeminent haiku poets in subsequent years but passed away on May 11th, 1956 at the young age of 51. His haiku were graceful, elegant, and refined. He had delicate sensibility and an accurate technique of sketch. His best friend, Kawabata Bohsha, praised him as "a born aristocrat in haiku literature."

The meaning of the above haiku is this: the death of Takashi will be compared to a petal of the magnificent peony fallen in the long history of haikai. The peony is a noble and splendid flower and often called "the king of flowers."

We have previously read Kyoshi's other mourning haiku for the deceased Suzuki Hanamino (see #47). In that haiku, we saw Kyoshi's rather personal sentiment for the departed. But here in this haiku, his more public sentiment for the sadness of the world of haiku is expressed from the viewpoint of the history of haiku.

No. 90

俳諧を守りの神の涼しさよ

Haikai o mamori no kami no suzushisa-yo

Literal translation:

Summer coolness of God
Blessing and nurturing
Haikai

Seasonal word: *suzushi*, cool (summer) [Coolness is what we feel in autumn, but we appreciate coolness the more during hot summer.]

Written in June, 1956, when Kyoshi was 82 years old.

This is one of the eight haiku Kyoshi wrote when he climbed Mt. Haguro in a *kago*. *Haikai* can be understood here to be almost the same as haiku. But we should not forget that it was Bashoh who long ago developed haikai into a high-minded literature.

More than three hundred years ago, Matsuo Bashoh, who is the most famous Haiku poet in the history of Japanese literature, wrote the following haiku:

How cool and serene –   (涼しさやほの三日月の羽黒山)
Haguro mountain under   (Suzushisa-ya hono-mikadsuki no Hagurosan)
Faint crescent moon

It is obvious that Kyoshi's haiku was written with Bashoh's haiku in mind.

Then who is this god? When I read Bashoh's <u>Oku-no-Hoso-Michi</u>, I reached the conclusion that this god must be Haguro-Gongen. The next question is: why is this god expressed as a "god protecting and nurturing *haikai?*"

When Bashoh visited Mt. Haguro, he held a haikai meeting at the temple there. I believe that Kyoshi's journey to Mt. Haguro in his later years must have been not only to trace Bashoh's route but also to embark on a pilgrimage to his spiritual world. Then he understood how serenely determined Bashoh was about haikai.

No. 91

蜘蛛に生れ網をかけねばならぬかな

Kumo ni are ami o kakeneba naranu-kana

Literal translation:

Born as a spider
No choice but to spin
His spider web!

Seasonal word: spider (summer)

This haiku was written on June 17th, 1956 at Kanoh-san Jinya-ji when Kyoshi was 82, in the last haiku meeting of the *Keiko-kai*, which lasted for three days.

Kyoshi was walking in the garden of the temple which had been swept clean of dirt, dust, and cobwebs. When he later returned, however, he found some new cobwebs had been spun. Although he was annoyed at first, he soon recognized that it was simply the spider's natural behavior.

In the first line of the above haiku, "Born as a spider," Kyoshi remarks on the fate of a spider. The second and third lines, "no choice but to spin his spider web" describe what a spider does, driven by its destiny. And the exclamation point, which is expressed in Japanese with the cutting word *kana*, shows Kyoshi's emotional attitude of accepting it with a sigh.

It shows that Kyoshi thinks the spider is on equal footing with human beings. With this understanding, this haiku comes to have deeper meaning—that is, Kyoshi sees himself reflected in the spider. He thinks that the spider, which has to keep weaving his cobweb, is just like him, who has to keep creating haiku and selecting and critiquing his pupils' haiku as long as he lives.

It also tells us more. We human beings are fated to subsist on many other animals and plants, just as a spider is fated to subsist on the bugs it traps in its web. We have to remember that spiders are not greedy, though. They don't want more than they need to live, nor do they make more than one cobweb at a time.

We cannot always avoid evil and wickedness in our life, but Kyoshi takes a positive view of human life. His view is that haiku is poetry "to sing of everything in nature, just as we sing of birds and flowers"(kachou-fuh-ei).

Of course, Kyoshi himself does not say anything like this. He might not have even considered this notion. But we are naturally inclined to think these things in our lingering echoes of this haiku. Why? Because this is the haiku of son-mon—the haiku of son-mon for a little spider, for the poet himself, for life itself, for God. A poem of only seventeen syllables may sometimes possess such eloquence because of its power of son-mon.

"Son-mon" is understood in Japanese as asking or saluting. When Kyoshi uses this word, however, it has a deeper meaning. For Kyoshi, son-mon can be best described as "empathetic intercommunication between living or nonliving things in the name of the Creator."

No. 92

楓林に落せし鬼の歯なるべし

Huhrin ni otoseshi oni no ha narubeshi

Literal translation:

This must be a tooth
Dropped by an old ogre
In the red maple woods

Seasonal word: maple (autumn)

Written in July, 1958, when Kyoshi was 83 years old.

This haiku is entitled "the Grave Mound of the Tooth." This "tooth grave" was built in Kanoh-san, Jinya-ji to worship a tooth Kyoshi lost.

I have been interested in this haiku for a long time but have not been satisfied with its interpretations. I selected it for this series in order to study and consider it once more. I would like to address three points I could not understand well.

First of all, I was deeply impressed by the Noh play-like image and charmed by the unique combination of an ogre and the scarlet maple woods. However, I could not find out which Noh it came from. Secondly, the maple woods in this haiku must be the woods with autumnal, scarlet-tinged leaves. This means the season should be autumn, although the haiku was written in July. Thirdly, this is one of three haiku written on the same occasion. The first haiku shows Kyoshi's embarrassment and bewilderment about having a "grave mound" for his tooth. On the other hand, in the above haiku, the poet does not really reveal his feelings about it. It seems that he did not dare to share his honest feelings about building it.

In another essay, Kyoshi confessed that he had not been very happy about the idea of building a tooth grave and that he finally acquiesced to having it built when he thought of the above haiku. He said that the image of the tooth as an old ogre dropped, wandering in the beautiful autumn maple woods soothed and comforted him. I now believe Kyoshi composed this haiku as a new Noh-play with the image of "the excursion for viewing scarlet maple leaves, *momiji-gari.*

No. 93

たぐひなき菊の契りとことほぎぬ

Taguinaki kiku no chigiri to kotohoginu

Literal translation:

Congratulation!
Peerless and eternal
Chrysanthemum vow

Seasonal word: *kiku*, chrysanthemum (autumn)

This haiku was written on October 7th, 1954, when Kyoshi was 80 years old.

This is the haiku Kyoshi dedicated to Chihara Sohshi and Adsumi Eiko to celebrate their wedding.

Chihara Sohshi was a young brain surgeon and one of the leading members of Harunakai of Kyoto University. He became the first editor-in-chief of the haiku monthly published by Hatano Soh-ha in 1953.

On the other hand, Eiko was famous as the heroine of Kyoshi's novel Story of Tsubakiko (Little Camellia). In 1945, the year World War II ended, Kyoshi visited Wadayama to meet the blind haiku poet, Adsumi Sogan, who had lost his sight due to a detached retina he suffered when he was studying at Doshisha University. With his hand on his young daughter Eiko's shoulder, the blind Sogan guided Kyoshi around his town. Kyoshi was charmed by Eiko's beautifully braided hair and quiet winsomeness (see # 64).

Three years later, upon graduating from the same university her late father once attended, she visited Kyoshi in Kamakura. Kyoshi was very much pleased to see the pretty, young Eiko. Later he gave her his beloved Japanese doll named 'Tubakiko (Little Camellia), which he had kept beside him.

After this Story of Tsubakiko was published, many haiku poets wished Eiko a happy marriage. This haiku of Kyoshi's is indeed a suitable, thoughtful, and heartfelt haiku to celebrate the wedding of Sohshi and Eiko.

No. 94

春潮や和寇の子孫汝と我

Shunchoh ya wakoh no shison nare to ware

Literal translation:

Spring tide
Descended from Japanese Pirates
You and I

Seasonal words: *shunchou*, Spring tide

Written in October, 1949, when Kyoshi was 75 years old.

This haiku was dedicated to Imai Goroh, the Mayor of Hashihama and the husband of Tsurujo, Kyoshi's niece. In 1945, at the very end of World War Ⅱ, the Imai family moved from Tokyo to Hashihama in Ehime prefecture. When the war ended, he became the Mayor of the town and worked there until 1955.

Kyoshi wrote the above haiku according to Goroh's wish to build a stone monument of Kyoshi's haiku in that town. This masterful poem reminds readers of the grand and dynamic tide along the straits of Kurushima and the history of that area.

However, when this haiku and the date of the opening ceremony for the monument were announced in the newspaper, there arose some opinions that the haiku "you and I are descendants of the Japanese pirates" was not suitable for the monument. A heated debate soon appeared in the newspaper, with strong opinions on both sides.

Worried about the situation, Kyoshi wrote a letter to his niece Tsurujo, offering to change the above haiku as follows

Spring tide!
Sea breams and young yellowtails and
You and I

He added that this alternative haiku could also be the poem of homage and praise for the grandeur of the spring tide of the strait.

In the end, the mayor and his wife Tsurujo insisted on Kyoshi's original haiku. It was their belief that the original haiku was best suited for the stone monument, as it told the history of the strait of Kurushima under the Sun.

No. 95

脱落し去り脱落し去り明の春

Datsuraku-shisari datsuraku-shisari ake-no-haru

Literal translation:

Freer and freer
As worldly attachments fall away –
The New Year's Day

Seasonal word: the New Year's day, *ake-no-haru*

This haiku was written in November of 1953, when Kyoshi was 78 years old. It is one of the haiku he wrote for the coming New Year in response to requests from newspapers and haiku monthlies.

Datsuraku is the key word of this haiku. Without understanding the meaning of this word, we will not be able to appreciate it. *Datsuraku* here is the abbreviation of *shinjin-datsuraku* (身心脱落) in the Zen sect of Buddhism. It may be roughly translated as "to free oneself from one's ego and from whatever attachment or tenacity of both the mind and body." I interpret this poem as the haiku of Kyoshi's experience of "Nirvana"— that is, the spiritual state of peace and happiness free from all attachments. The repetition of *datsuraku-shisari* in the haiku could be interpreted as the repetition of his experiences.

Kyoshi neither practiced any religious training as an ascetic nor tried to sit in religious meditations of Zen-Buddhism. However, he deeply study its philosophies. He recited *Kachoh-fuh-ei* as the Name of Amida Buddha and conversed in his heart with all living and non-living things he met for writing haiku—that is, *son-mon*. Through repeating *son-mon* he realized that there is no difference between his life and the lives of birds or flowers, and that we all share the life of the great Creator.

Nirvana was what Kyoshi attained after his life-long *son-mon*.

Note: In the religion of Buddhism, Nirvana is the state of peace and happiness that a person achieves after giving up all personal desires.

No. 96

傷一つ翳一つなき初御空

Kizu hitotsu kage hitotsu naki hatsu-misora

Literal translation

Neither a scar
Nor an impurity
Sky of New Year's Day

Seasonal word: Sky of New Year's Day, *Hatsu-misora*

This haiku was written on December 21st, 1958 when Kyoshi was 84 years old.

Kyoshi passed away on April 8th, 1959. So the above haiku was his last New Year haiku.

"The sky with no scar or impurity" can be interpreted as "a beautiful, perfect sky." What a pure and magnificent view of the universe he was able to appreciate on his last New Year's day!

Around 1917, Kyoshi wrote the following unique and very famous haiku:

初空や大悪人虚子の頭上に

Hatsuzora ya dai-akunin Kyoshi no zujoh ni

New Year's sky
Above the head of Kyoshi
The great wicked man

When he looked up at the pure, heavenly sky of the New Year's day, Kyoshi realized how wicked and full of worldly desires he was. However, he acknowledged and embraced this truth about himself. He continued along his arduous journey toward self-discovery and self-acceptance by repeating *son-mon* in haiku. *Son-mon*, which is sometimes pronounced '*zon-mon*,' has often been referred to in the essays of this series. In short, *son-mon* is "asking, greeting, addressing, and talking to anybody or anything in nature." At the end of his life, Kyoshi was able to engage in *son-mon* with the great Creator.

In haiku #96, all we see is the perfect, pure sky of New Year's Day. Under that sky we will not see Kyoshi because he is now free from worldly existence, standing on the other side of the "world of good and evil or right and wrong."

No. 97

悪なれば色悪よけれ老の春

Aku nareba iroaku yokere oi-no-haru

Literal translation:

If you ask me about aku
I would rather be iro-aku in kabuki –
Spring of senescence

Seasonal word: *oi-no-haru*, spring of senescence (the New Year)

This haiku was written in January, 1953 when Kyoshi was 80 years old.

Iro-aku is a kabuki term which means "the prototypical handsome villain who is the hero's nemesis." This haiku has a unique, interesting preface as follows:

Kyohgoku Kiyoh says there are some who are wicked but effective and others who are not.

The meaning of this haiku could be something like this: If I have to be asked about *aku*, I would rather be a handsome villain against the hero in kabuki.

Mashita Kitaroh, Kyoshi's son-in-law, once remarked that Kyoshi's haiku were majestic and noble—not only wide but also deep—and that they were neither compromising nor constrained. This comment seems to have the same tone embodied in the phrase *aku ga kiku*, which, roughly translated, means "wicked but effective." This haiku might be Kyoshi's reaction to the above remarks.

Now we have to remember that *aku* in this essay is essentially different from *aku* we referred to in Kyoshi's haiku written in 1917 (see #96). In that haiku, *aku* could be said to mean the fundamental "evil" rooted in the absurdity of human existence.

In this haiku, *aku*, in a sense, means "power (strength, intensity, or toughness)." I should also point out that Kyoshi's understanding of wickedness had been wiped out in the years between these two haiku. Indeed, Kyoshi is powerful in his haiku.

However I cannot agree totally with Mashita Kitaroh. I hesitate to accept what Kitaroh said about Kyoshi's haiku because I feel his assessment of Kyoshi falls short. Let's look at some of the haiku we have already read in previous chapters.

A frozen butterfly / Will fly after / Its own soul (#25)

Through the trunk of / This plum tree of red blossoms / Crimson must be running (#26)

In the daylight / Stars are glowing; / Mushrooms are growing (#58)

Old year, new year – / Just like *boh* / Carrying through (#61)

Reading these haiku, I am awestruck by Kyoshi's metaphorical originality. Why? I think it is because these haiku reveal universal truths. Could it be that the essence of Kyoshi's haiku is the "truth?" When we replace *aku* with *shin*, (the truth), indeed the truth is pervasive and powerful.

No. 98

白梅に住み古りたりといふのみぞ

Hakubai ni sumihuritari to yuu nomi-zo

Literal translation:

Old plum tree –
White blossoms in bloom;
You and I have lived too long

Seasonal word: plum blossoms (spring)
Kyoshi wrote this haiku on February 23rd in 1959 at the age of 85.

This is one of nineteen haiku written on the same day. The old plum tree in front of Kyoshi's house produced innumerable blossoms that spring. It was the tree all his visitors admired for its delicate white blossoms. That particular year, however, the plum tree bore so many blossoms that it seemed to appear chaotic and wild. Kyoshi described it as "messy" and "wild" in his other haiku.

Kyoshi writes in his book <u>Road to Haiku</u> (*Haiku-e-no-Michi*) as follows:

> The spiritual life is a deep tide and poems are ripples on its surface. If you read my <u>Haiku Diary</u> (*Ku-Nikki*) deep and well, it will show you waves and ripples on the surface of my life. If you read it profoundly and carefully, you may understand my life through these ripples.

For Kyoshi, life is not the subject of his haiku but rather the womb from which his haiku are born (created). Human life, as well as the lives of plants and flowers, is the manifestation of all living things in the great universe. The life and death of a human being, as well as the blooming and dying of a flower, are merely phenomena of the universe.

No. 99

春の山屍をうめて空しかり

Haru no yama kabane o umete munashi-kari

Literal translation:

Spring mountain
With the corpse buried —
How insignificant and small

Seasonal word: spring mountain

This haiku was written on March 30th, 1959, at a Kuyohkai haiku meeting in Kamakura. Kyoshi was 85 years old.

On the day of that haiku meeting, cherry blossoms and camellias were in full bloom in the foothills in Kamakura. A strong wind in what might be called a spring storm was blowing, and the wind roared in Genji-yama. Understanding the circumstances under which this haiku was created, the corpse referred to in this haiku must be that of the shogun Minamoto-no-Yoritomo buried in the foothills of Kamakura.

Let's see what Kyoshi thinks about the death of human beings from "The Road to Haiku" written in his latest years. He writes as follows:

...I have been thinking about the human life and also about the changing of the four seasons, such as opening and falling of flowers. I now look at the birth and death of human beings as just phenomena of the universe, just like the life and death of flowers. The changing of the four seasons is passing us, making great sound, rushing toward us like surging tidal waves. We are living and passing away in that roar and waves.

For Kyoshi, Kamakura on that day must have seemed like a symbol of the throbbing universe. Compared with this dynamic spring mountain, the corpse of Yoritomo buried there seems so insignificant. Actually, the grave of Shogun Yoritomo became a part of Genji-yama only after seven hundred and fifty years. Even an epoch-making matter like the burial of the historical hero Yoritomo is a small thing in the universe.

Two days after he wrote the above haiku, Kyoshi was stricken by a cerebral hemorrhage and passed away on April 8th. He was buried in the graveyard of Juhuku-ji in Genjiyama in Kamakura. These situations suggest that Kyoshi wrote the above haiku because of his premonition about his death and that this corpse is meant to be Kyoshi's.

However, after reading all the other haiku Kyoshi wrote in the same haiku meeting, I could find no other indication that Kyoshi felt any sign of his death.

It is quite another question, though, whether Kyoshi subconsciously felt a sign of his death. This is an eternal question.

No. 100

独り句の推敲をして遅き日を

Hitori ku no suikou o shite osoki hi o

Literal translation:

In your solitude
Honing and perfecting your haiku –
On a slow spring day

Seasonal word: a slow spring day (a subtitle of a long spring day)

This is Kyoshi's last haiku. In his haiku notebook, there are six haiku written on March 30th,1959, including the one we talked about in the previous chapter. After a little space, there is this haiku written in pencil, with the preface "For the seventeenth memorial day of the death of Saint Kubutsu."

Saint Kubutu is the twenty-third Superintendent priest of Higashi Honganji. He had studied haiku since his youth and had been friends with Kyoshi for a long time.

This haiku has been interpreted as Kyoshi himself going over his own haiku again and again on a long spring day. When I chose this haiku for the hundredth piece of this series, I thought it a good opportunity to investigate afresh how it originated and to think it over again more deeply.

In April 1959, at Higashi Honganji, the 17th memorial day of saint Kubutsu was to be held for seven days. On the fifth evening, Kyoshi was invited to give a lecture on Kubutsu. Because Kyoshi was uncertain about his own health condition, he asked his son Toshio to read the manuscript he had prepared for this occasion. He also told his son the following important story about Kubutsu:

Kubutsu had once asked Kyoshi to travel around Japan to talk about haiku, but Kyoshi, who did not feel up to doing so, asked Hekigotou to go instead. Thus, with Kubutsu's financial support, Hekigotou traveled all around Japan, using this opportunity to galvanize his new movement of haiku. Kubutsu, who did not approve of this, cut off all relations with haiku poets and started the page called *"Ware-wa-ware"* ("I am myself") in his haiku monthly.

It is obvious now that this haiku is what is called *zohtohku*, a greeting haiku, in which Kyoshi addresses the deceased Kubutsu. When Kyoshi says "in your solitude," it is a reference to Kubutsu's column "I am Myself."

We can appreciate Kyoshi's reverence and friendship for Kubutsu, who must be following his own path in *gokuraku* (Buddhist heaven).

AUTHOR'S NOTES

Teiko Inabata

Eight years and four months have passed since I started to write *"Hundred Haiku of Kyoshi"* for <u>Haiku Kenkyu</u>, a haiku monthly. It was completed in April, 2006 and the book, <u>Hundred Haiku of Kyoshi</u>, was published in September of that year.

It had been my great pleasure to continue writing articles every month, thanks to the kindness and encouragement I received from the editor and readers. I would especially like to express my sincerest gratitude to Mr. Inaoka Hisashi who was in charge of researching all resources and reference works.

I am now looking back on the days I was writing <u>Hundred Haiku of Kyoshi</u> as if it were what someone else had done. Nowadays I am busy again with innumerable works and wonder how I was able to have managed the necessary time to concentrate on those essays. I even tell myself that they might have been the outcome of sheer enthusiasm or even madness.

It was painstaking to choose only one hundred haiku from the enormous volume of haiku Kyoshi wrote throughout his life. Indeed, there are many that seem easy to write about or to interpret, and those which have note-worthy context or background information. On the other hand, there are many which are sometimes difficult, obscure or incomprehensible, and those that everyone agrees are good haiku and yet impossible to discuss in limited space.

At the beginning I chose the easiest and most accessible haiku, but soon I realized that I should choose haiku in chronological order, and that the month they were written should fit the month of publication of the magazine. I think I was able to adhere to this guideline fairly closely.

By pursuing Kyoshi's haiku chronologically, I noticed, very vaguely at the beginning but more distinctly later, that I came to see the inner side of Kyoshi. I reached the conclusion that the change or growth of Kyoshi's haiku was nothing but the deepening of his eyes, that is, deepening of his idea and thinking. As my afterword of this book I would like to write about Kyoshi's development as a *haijin* and a philosopher.

I am afraid there has been an established opinion that Kyoshi's haiku have not changed through his life. But Kyoshi's haiku of his later years of life are obviously different from those of his younger days.

Characteristic of young Kyoshi was his 'animistic' eye as his mentor Shiki once said. Shiki says that Kyoshi looks at plants the same way he looks at human beings. He has an inborn ability to sympathize with or respond object and be one with it.

A second characteristic of Kyoshi is his consciousness of ego, which was nurtured in him by his higher education in Meiji era. Kyoshi seems to have written haiku, swaying between these two (characteristics, his animism and his ego). His first haiku anthology titled *"Go-Hyakku"*, <u>Five-Hundred Haiku</u> is full of masterpieces of his earlier life.

In 1917 when Kyoshi was 43years old, he attended the funeral of his (eldest) brother. When he looked up at the face of Amitabha Buddha, he encountered the idea that the life of all living things are equal and same, and could be the life given from Amitabha Buddha.

In 1928, at the age of fifty-five, he used his famous phrase"Kachou-fuh-ei", for the first time, Kyoshi included human beings in this phrase *Kachou* (flowers and birds). Moreover, *fuh-ei* (to sing of) was also given the meaning "to praise and glorify" which was not in the dictionary.

Eventually Kyoshi said "haiku is a poem of *son-mon*" which was named for "saluting", one of the characteristics of old haikai. This *son-mon* 'saluting' has been given a wider and deeper meaning in Kyoshi's haiku. Haiku poets have *son-mon* with any being in nature from little pebbles, to mountains, rivers, clouds in the sky, or even supernatural beings like Gods, or other human being, even with the poet himself. It was during the years Kyoshi was living in Komoro in Shinshu during and after the World War II, that he deepened his *son-mon*. We can trace it in the following haiku of this book such as the numbers 47, 52, 56, 57, 58, 59, 70 and 95. In number 67, you will see his experiences of mysticism.

Kyoshi, then, reached the philosophy *Gokuraku-no-bungaku*, 'the literature of paradise'. He embodies this thought in the haiku No.95 where he reached through his repeated experiences of what is called nirvana. Kyoshi was finally able to cast off his 'ego'. You will see this change in his haiku in No. 84, 88, 91 and 96.

At this point in his development you have the image of Kyoshi, free from any worldly attachment, talking with nature, accepting everything as it is. He accepts both life and death as they are.

I feel Kyoshi addressing to us all: we are not only enjoying comfort for a while by writing haiku, but also we can live in paradise forever freeing ourselves from our ego.

Modern haiku is, in a word, the haiku of ego. Ego is the product of modern metaphysics.

Looking over the world of haiku after Kyoshi, those who exclaimed that time was their own seem somehow insignificant by comparison. It is obvious that western metaphysics has collapsed. Structuralism has been rising. Those waves will eventually reach the modern literature of our country, and later the world of haiku.

Teiko Inabata, July 2006

ABOUT THE AUTHOR

TEIKO INABATA, author of <u>100 Works of Kyoshi</u>, is the third President of Japan's largest haiku society, *Hototogisu*, founded by her grandfather, Takahama Kyoshi, about hundred and twenty years ago. Since childhood, she has been familiar with haiku, influenced by her grandfather, Kyoshi. In 1949, at the age of eighteen, when she quit her studies at Sacred Heart College because of pleurisy, she decided to focus on haiku and live as a haiku poet.

Every summer in those days, Kyoshi would conduct haiku meetings for young students of Tokyo University, Kyoto University and Gakushuin College beside Lake Yamanaka-ko. Teiko attended all these meetings and studied haiku with those excellent young students. (Those same young students who studied haiku with Teiko in her youth would later help and support her in establishing the Japan Traditional Haiku Society.) She also followed Kyoshi, Toshio (her father) and Tatsuko (her aunt), who were also famous haiku poets, in their haiku journeys. Teiko, as she wrote once, learned and acquired a great deal of skill and knowledge about writing haiku as well as the soul of haiku.

Teiko became a Catholic when she was a high-school student. She married Inabata Junzoh, also a Catholic, in 1956. Even now, she goes to church every Sunday when she is not traveling. It is a great wonder how Teiko accepts and harmonizes Catholic doctrine with the praise of nature central to *kachou-fuh-ei*. Judging from what we understand from her haiku, we feel there is, at the bottom of her *kachou-fuh-ei*, glorification of nature, or rather, glorification for the Creator of Nature.

The best way to invite you into Teiko's world is to show you some of her haiku, translated in English.

| 春光を砕きては波かがやかに | Shunkoh o kudakitewa nami kagayaka ni |

Breaking spring light
Waves shine
Bright and brilliant

| 海見えて風花光るものとなる | Umi miete kazahana hikaru mono to naru |

Light snow begins to
Flicker and glisten, as comes
The sea into view

淡々と冬日は波を渡りけり　　　Usu-usu-to fuyuhi wa nami o watarikeri

    Faint and frail
    Winter sun is crossing
    On waves

明るさは海よりのもの野水仙　　Akarusa wa umi yori no mono nozuisen

    Shimmering brilliance
    Comes from the sea –
    A field of wild narcissus

月の波消え月の波生まれつつ　　Tsuki no nami kie tsuki no nami umaretsutsu

    Waves of moon light dying –
    Waves of moon light
    Are being born

Disasters and horrible experiences such as the air raid at the end of World War II (which burned her house to ashes), her lonesome days in the dormitory in Tokyo right after the war, her sense of frustration at quitting college because of illness, her grief over her father's death and, soon afterwards, the death of her beloved husband caused Teiko to open her eyes and soul to "the light." Because Teiko appreciated even the slightest light in the darkness, one might refer to her as the "haiku poet of light."

Teiko made a great contribution to the internationalization of the haiku by visiting China in 1982, Munich and Vienna in 1985, Munich again and the Vatican City in 1987. She and other haiku poets were also presented to the Pope at Vatican Palace and had a haiku meeting at the Vatican embassy.

In April 1987, she established the Japan Traditional Haiku Society and assumed the role of President. In 1989, she held the first International Haiku Conference at Lake Yamanakako. Since then, the society has held a conference every two years. The fifth conference was held in the spring of 2008 in Ashiya-city.

In 2000, right after the great earthquake in Kobe, Teiko established the Kyoshi Memorial Museum next to her own house in Ashiya and became the president. Safe and sound in the fireproof, quakeproof storage building of the Museum are precious historical literary treasures: all the memorabilia, important history, Kyoshi's out-of-print books, letters, diaries and journals, *shikishi*, *tanzaku*, and manuscripts not only by Kyoshi but also by great men-of-letters such as Shiki, Hekigotoh, Sohseki and many others.

At the top of the *Hototogisu* world, Teiko does her best to judge the innumerable numbers of haiku sent from the members of *Hototogisu* and to attend the haiku meetings held all over Japan, leaving her great footprints nationally and internationally. In 2005, she handed over *zatuei-senja* (the judge of the haiku submitted from the members) to her son, Inabata Kohtaroh, who is the vice-president of *Hototogisu*.

To close this essay, here are some examples of Teiko's haiku (her choice):

空といふ自由鶴舞ひ止まざるは   Sora to yuu jiyuh tsuru mai-yamazaru-wa
    Freedom in the sky –
    Cranes will not stop
    Flying

長き夜の苦しみを解き給ひしや   Nagaki yo no kurushimi o toki tamaishi-ya
    Might God have let him   Is it Grace that has now
    Free from his agony   Released him from the agony
    In long autumnal night   Long autumnal night

さゆらぎは開く力よ月見草   Sayuragi wa hiraku chikara-yo tsukimi-soh
    Wavering and flickering
    Impetus to unfurl
    Evening primrose

Hisashi Inaoka and Aya Nagayama